Janie   Att. 1

MW00884617

"I Saw Heaven!"

Life Changing Conversations with My
Brother after His Near Death Experience

Patti Miller Dunham

Xulon
PRESS

Copyright © 2010 by Patti Miller Dunham

"I Saw Heaven!"
Life Changing Conversations with My Brother
after His Near Death Experience
by Patti Miller Dunham

Printed in the United States of America

ISBN 9781609573690

www.xulonpress.com

Lovingly dedicated to my brother,
Richard E. Miller
(1937-2004)

Contents

Acknowledgements

To my family members and friends who encouraged me to write this book, may I say that without you, I wouldn't have been able to have the insight, courage, and stamina to see God's hand so clearly in all that happened during this extraordinary, life-changing experience.

First, thank you to each of my precious family members, including my mother, Mable Miller, my daughter Natalie, son-in-law Richard, grandsons Keylan and Dayton, sisters-in-law Pat and Mary, and my brother Richard's children—Steve, Cathy, Tom, Aaron and Andy.

Next, it is so important for me to express my gratitude to Pat and Rick, who have been much more than friends for 25 years—I couldn't have made it without you!

Nor could I have made it without my wonderful Monday morning Bible study sisters. You kept me going when I couldn't do it by myself.

Mountains of appreciation also go to Betty, Boyce, Carol, Carolyn, Cassie, Cheri, Christopher, Don, Jana, Judy, Linda,

Maranda, Mary, Peggy, Penny, Tom, Victorya and Viney, for I am certain that without you, the words on the following pages would have stayed largely unwritten.

To so many more who are unnamed (but immensely appreciated), I am grateful from the bottom of my heart.

Finally, to Darryl, my sincere thanks and deep appreciation for your writing skills and encouragement, and to Karen goes a bouquet of appreciation for your seasoned advice. Without our God-ordained meeting, this book would have remained in my journal and my heart.

Note from the Author

During the period of time prior to and during the months this extraordinary event took place, I was going through a very rough season.

Suffice it to say that I have gone through much—I have been hurt, I've hurt others, and I have hurt myself.

During the process of writing this book and reliving some of those times, I have made a conscious choice to avoid causing additional pain to others or myself by recounting all those details.

Complete forgiveness has come as I have realized that these incidents were used by God for good in my life, though I certainly didn't understand it at the time. And I can also truly say that I would go through each again to gain the knowledge of God's wonderful love and grace.

I have learned that hurting people hurt people. That knowledge has made forgiveness not only possible, but necessary.

I can honestly say that today I have no hate, resentment, bitterness, anger, or desire to expose others' wrongs in this book. If I do bring an incident up to give the reader more clarity in a situation, I have done my best to keep the person's identity protected by changing names and locations.

Because of the life-changing process I went through, as expressed in this book, I have reached such a sweet place of forgiveness. It is wonderful to say that I have been forgiven, and I have totally forgiven.

Just as God did in the Bible's Old Testament for His children, He has delivered me from bondage—which I was totally unaware of—brought me into a good place, given me a life of faith and peace, and I am so deeply grateful. I will give God all the glory, honor and praise forever.

Who knows what lies ahead, but I can candidly say that the hurts and challenges of the past are far behind me, and I cannot begin to describe what this means to me.

Again, the peace that I possess now is why I have left many details and names out of this book, choosing instead to focus on the conversations with my brother and the new life I have received as a result.

Introduction

Then I saw a new heaven and a new earth, for the first heaven and the first earth had passed away, and there was no longer any sea. I saw the Holy City, the new Jerusalem, coming down out of heaven from God, prepared as a bride beautifully dressed for her husband. And I heard a loud voice from the throne saying, "Now the dwelling of God is with men, and he will live with them. They will be his people, and God himself will be with them and be their God. He will wipe every tear from their eyes. There will be no more death or mourning or crying or pain, for the old order of things has passed away.". . . .The twelve gates were twelve pearls, each gate made of a single pearl. The great street of the city was of pure gold, like transparent glass. I did not see a temple in the city, because the Lord God Almighty and the Lamb are its temple.—Revelation 21:1-4; 21-22

"I saw heaven!"

Those three words were the last I would have expected to hear from my brother Richard. He had been in a coma for six days. When I finally was able to go into his room for my allotted ten minutes, I had planned to encourage him and cherish the precious moments, knowing it would perhaps be the last I would spend with him.

Then he said those words—and more.

These words, so unthinkable from a brother who had lived most of his life addicted to alcohol.

These words, so unexpected from my quiet, plainspoken, straightforward, unassuming brother.

These words, the beginning of an entirely new relationship with my brother that would shake me to my soul's core and change my world forever.

"I saw heaven!"

CঙԸO

August 27, 2001. The call came from the Southeast Missouri Hospital in Cape Girardeau. Through my sobs, I tried to hear all the details: "Your brother Richard . . . congestive heart failure . . . in a coma . . . intensive care . . . on life support."

Then came the final sentence that shocked me beyond words.

"All the family has been called," the voice said. "He's probably not going to make it. If you want to see him before he dies, you need to come right away."

It was the worst time for me to leave. I was dealing with business and personal challenges, but I knew I couldn't delay. I immediately dropped everything and packed enough for a few days, pausing during a moment of extreme sadness as I pulled a black suit and shoes from my closet, just in case.

I hurried to Missouri from my home in a suburb of Dallas, Texas. Everything was a blur—the waiting room, the family and friends gathered together, the worried faces, the latest news. We staged our vigil for what we expected to be the last hours of my brother Richard Miller's life. We silently prayed, cried, tried to be courageous, and called other family members and friends to relay the scant details we could glean from the ICU nurses.

The doomsday news continued. Then the unthinkable happened. Richard started getting better. Eventually the life support was removed. He kept improving.

Finally, after the breathing tubes were removed, the physicians decided to let each member of the immediate family go in to see him for just ten minutes at a time.

"He's very, very sick," we were told. "He is very weak. Don't expect too much from him."

Mary, my sister-in-law went in to be with him first, then his grown children. Finally it was time that my mother and I could go in and spend our ten minutes with him.

Before we went in, I kept trying to prepare myself for the moment when I would see him. I didn't want him to see alarm or sadness in my eyes or face. I mainly wanted to encourage him.

I thought, he's going to be so weak and unable to talk. I'm just going to tell him that I love him, hold his hand and assure him that I would continue to pray for him and tell him how well he's doing. I rehearsed the words several times.

When we went into the room, we stood there looking at him. Mother stood at the foot of his bed, lovingly touching her sixty-three-year-old son. She had birthed him, nurtured him, and loved him, even through the darkest decades.

I went to his side, taking his hand, looking at the brother, six years older than me, with whom I had so little in common.

"I love you, Richard," I heard my voice saying the words I had prepared. "I've been praying for you, and I'm going to keep praying. You are doing well, and you are going to make it."

I could tell that he could hear my encouraging words, but I didn't expect him to respond. I knew that he could barely talk since he had been taken off the breathing machine. The others who had been with him before us told us that he was very weak.

It was difficult to see my brother so very, very frail, but I was so glad to see him. In fact, I was still amazed that we were able to be with him at all after the coma and warnings.

Then something changed. Everything about him seemed to change. My brother looked at me. His face lit up. I looked into his eyes, and they were the most beautiful crystal-blue color I had ever seen.

"I saw heaven!" he exclaimed. "It's beautiful!"

He kept saying that over and over.

"It's beautiful! I saw this huge pearl gate. It's huge!"

My mind could barely grasp these totally unexpected words I was hearing, yet immediately I thought, "My brother went to heaven!"

I didn't even have the time or energy to be skeptical. I knew that Richard wasn't the kind of person who easily got excited. Most of the time he wasn't talkative. He wouldn't have said it if it weren't true.

And he kept saying it: "It's beautiful! It's *beau*-tiful!"

He mentioned the pearl gate again—"It's huge. *Huge!*"

Tears were streaming down our faces—Mother's, Richard's, and mine. Then I realized that I couldn't remember ever seeing my brother weep in front of me. That is when the depths of what he was saying struck me.

I knew it was true; the man lying in the bed was acting so differently from the brother I knew. I felt the presence of God as he was sharing his truly remarkable experience. I felt as if I was standing on holy ground in that intensive care room.

Through his tears, he said, "I didn't see God, but He told me I had to go back because He has more work for me to do."

Something had happened to my brother! I had prayed for him for years. He hadn't seemed too spiritual to me! And now God had let him see heaven! I was amazed.

Then, even as I tried to comprehend what he was saying, the ICU attendants came to say it was time to go.

⋙⋘

After leaving the hospital that evening, my Mother and I opened the Bible to the book of Revelation and began to read the description of heaven found in chapter 21—the new heaven and new earth, the Holy City, the twelve gates of twelve pearls, each gate made from a single pearl, and the city's great street made of pure gold.

Mother and I looked at each other. Inwardly we knew that Richard had actually seen that "*beau*–tiful place," as he had described it. As difficult as it was to believe, it was true, yet neither of us knew how to react to what we had heard, except to accept it and rejoice that something so wonderful had happened to him.

I became a Christian back in 1969 and had been very involved in church most of the time since then. While I had been glad when I heard Richard finally received the Lord Jesus into his heart years after me, he had never seemed too religious afterward. I had been glad he had become a Christian, but we still had little in common—and sadly, we weren't close.

૭ૐૐ

Richard was six years older than me, so we were in vastly different worlds during our childhood years in our small Missouri hometown. Our lives had taken different paths since those early years. So, even after he continued to recover from the congestive heart failure in 2001 and eventually went home, we didn't talk a lot. He never discussed the subject of heaven with me again during the next few years, and I didn't feel comfortable pressing him for details.

Yet I saw an immediate difference in him. When I went back to Missouri to be with my family for holidays, before meals we would stand and hold hands, and always before we ate he would ask me to pray.

After the life-changing event during his coma, Richard never asked me to pray again. He prayed, and as he did, my brother talked to God as though He was Someone whom he knew intimately and personally. It was clear to everyone that a change had happened in his life.

Still, we weren't all that close, though we talked occasionally. Mostly it was surface things. So what began on December 9, 2003, more than two years after he told us he had seen heaven, made what happened from that point forward even more astounding.

Back in 2001 in the Missouri Intensive Care Unit, when my brother talked of seeing heaven, he also said, "I didn't see God, but He told me I had to go back because He has more work for me to do."

Little did I know part of the work planned for him was his own sister.

CঙৎৎO

Time passed. Then in December of 2003, I found myself in one of the deepest valleys of my life. Even as the world continued to struggle through the uncertainty and financial downturn after 9/11, I was having my own challenges that were threatening to tear me apart.

I had been through difficult circumstances before, but this was worse in many ways. I soon realized that I was lost in bleak darkness, waiting for any glimpse of light, and I wasn't sure I would ever be able to climb out from the murky pit.

I kept saying, "I only want God's will." I asked people to pray that I would know God's will. I did not want to make wrong choices and suffer unnecessarily. Still, I didn't seem to be able to find the right answers.

Then a light in the darkness appeared before me. Richard called one morning, out of the blue.

"Mother has told me about some of the things you are going through," he said, "so I just wanted to talk with you for a few minutes."

It started that simply and unexpectedly. It was the first of eighteen precious early morning conversations that would absolutely rock my world as I learned eternal wisdom from the most unexpected source—my brother.

Those conversations continued from time to time for the next eight months, as I poured out my feelings and kept a journal of everything that was spoken. The pages of those notebooks have since become a priceless legacy for me, the jottings of a journey that would transform my life forever. Through each of the conversations, then writing what transpired in my journal, I sensed that I was getting something so simple, clear and life-changing that it had to be from heaven.

Since then, as I have shared those written remembrances with people, I have received encouragement to put those precious memories into a book that many others may enjoy and learn from the straightforward principles I received from God through Richard.

At the end of each chapter is a section entitled "Conversations and Reflections" to help personalize your own journey, as well as a prayer that may be helpful to you in your own conversations with God.

That, simply stated, is my purpose for the pages you now hold in your hands. May you be as touched by heaven as I was touched. May you find the life-changing truths as I did during these conversations with my brother, Richard.

1

GOD'S WILL:
December 9, 2003

❧❧❧

"For my thoughts are not your thoughts, neither are your ways my ways, declares the Lord." —Isaiah 55:8

The conversation about heaven with my brother Richard happened on August 27, 2001. From that point forward we didn't talk a lot. As in the past, we talked a few times a year, but most of the time I did all the talking. He mostly said one-liners: "Yep. Nope. Okay. Bye."

Those conversations reflected our relationship. Older brother. Kid sister. We had very little in common except parents. We had always seemed to live in worlds that were poles apart.

Even though we grew up in a *Mayberry RFD*-like town in Missouri—population 3000, give or take a few—we grew

23

up very differently. I was six years younger, but anyone who has grown up with that gap in ages knows how significant it can be. It was for Richard and me.

For me, Dexter was a safe, protected place to live. From the time I started first grade, I walked across town from our house to the elementary school on Elm Street. There was no fear. My parents, Russell and Mable Miller, didn't even have keys to the locks on the doors to our house. My parents were well-respected in the town. My father worked as office manager for a trucking company. My mother was a volunteer at church, bridge player and a homemaker who kept things spotless and perfect.

Throughout the next few years, all my activities centered around school, piano lessons, voice lessons, my friends, and the Methodist church. I loved being part of everything that happened in my hometown. I was always singing—weddings, funerals, teas, and many school functions. I was a cheerleader in junior high, but in high school focused on being a twirler and majorette.

For Richard, our hometown was a different experience. He was affected by things that I never saw. We grew up in the same home and community, but went two diverse directions. He started drinking when he was a teenager, an addiction that would control much of his life for decades to come. He went to barber school in Denver, then he ended up in our home town as a barber, and eventually he bought a floundering barber supply business in a nearby Missouri town and turned it around. He put salespeople on the road and kept growing the company. The barber and beauty supply business he reclaimed continues to be successful to this day. He had a wonderful wife and three beautiful children. Still, the drinking got worse and worse, controlling virtually everything he did and eventually destroying his first marriage.

I had taken a different path. I graduated from high school in 1961, and then my friend Judy asked me to come and visit her. We had gone to school together since the first grade, but her family had moved to Texas when she was a high school junior.

Judy and her family came back to our hometown to visit, and I rode back with them to Fort Worth, 573 miles to the southwest. I had never been to a big city by myself in my whole life. When I took the train back to Missouri, I had already decided to take a job back in Texas.

And thus, more than forty years passed, with Richard and I living our own lives, connected by genes, parents, and small-town childhood experiences, but sharing little else. I had been touched by what he had said when he came out of the coma, but even after that we didn't talk to or see each other often since we lived quite a distance from each other.

Then, on Tuesday, December 9, 2003—more than four decades, several jobs, two business ownerships, fortunes built and lost, two long-term-but-failed marriages, one beautiful daughter, a wonderful son-in-law and two special grandchildren later—I received the fateful phone call from my brother, Richard.

It had been more than two years since Richard's bedside revelation about seeing heaven. I had remembered then, through his tears, he had said, "I didn't see God, but He told me I had to go back because He has more work for me to do."

When he said those words, I would have never thought in a million years that the unfinished work included me. That all changed with the first phone conversation just a few weeks prior to Christmas 2003. The subsequent phone calls would revolutionize my life.

ଓ୫୦

"Mother told me what's going on with you," he began, referring to the emotional earthquakes I was experiencing, "and I just wanted to call you."

It was out of the blue. As mentioned previously (but it bears repeating), Richard and I talked maybe three times a year, and I did all the talking. My brother's side of the conversations usually consisted of monosyllables.

By this time he had been sober for fifteen years. He had become a Christian earlier and tried going to church, but in order to stay free from alcohol, his church became Alcoholics Anonymous. I never thought very much of that. I had always thought he needed to be in a "real" church.

I was the one who had always attended church. I was the one who had studied my Bible and prayed all my life. I had attended lots of retreats and Bible studies, as well as leading Bible studies and speaking at retreats. I certainly didn't think that my brother had any background or information that could help me through the challenges I faced.

How wrong I was!

CGSO

When the first phone conversation began, I didn't know exactly what Richard knew about all that was happening with me. Frankly, as I shared a few things with Richard, I was admittedly waiting for him to say, "You know, you just need to get over this. Try to work it out and live happily ever after."

Lots of people had said similar things.

I listened to Richard's response. I wanted to see if he would downplay what I was going through. If I sensed that he was just going to brush it off or treat it lightly, I would be nice, but I would quickly close off that conversation. My heart was in so much pain that I couldn't take anyone treating it lightly.

While I was testing him, he seemed to be actually listening.

I'm sure I was testing him.

"Patti," he said, "I don't know anything about the other people in your life, and you don't, either. You don't know their life from when they were younger."

I didn't know that my brother was actually talking about himself.

He continued, "You don't know about how they grew up or their experiences. So you can't judge them, but you don't have to live with those situations. Only God knows what is in the hearts of other people. Only God knows about them. And they and God are going to have to work this out. He was referring to the sense of rejection I felt due to my discovery that my husband had a secret long-time addiction that he had hidden from me.

I couldn't believe this was coming from my brother. These were the most words I had ever heard at one time from him. What he was saying made sense. I kept listening.

"This is their deal," he pointed out. "This is between them and God, and you shouldn't even try to figure it out. You can't fix others. The best thing you can do is to stay out of their business. Let God take care of it."

Instead of judging me or trying to make light of what I was going through, Richard's words began setting me free.

I told him, "I just don't know what to do," as I described this situation I was facing.

I was saying it with such a sick feeling in my stomach. I felt so stupid and gullible. Here I'd been duped again. You can't feel any lower than when you feel as if you've been tricked, deceived, and betrayed all over again. Not once, but twice.

I said, "I want to do what God wants me to do. I want God's will. I don't know whether I should do one thing or another."

Richard listened to me for a few moments, and then he finally said, "Patti, you don't want God's will."

I said, "I do, too!"

He said, "No, you don't."

"I do, too!"

"No, you don't."

We argued like children, brother and sister, as we used to do in our hometown.

Finally he asked, "Do you want me to tell you how I know you don't really want God's will?"

I thought, how in the world does he know what he's talking about? Look, I'm the one who has walked with God for over thirty years. I'm the one who has been reading the Bible and going to church. Who are you to tell me anything about the Christian walk? You've spent your life as an alcoholic! And now you are telling me that I don't really want to do God's will?

I wouldn't have said those words out loud, but they expressed what I was feeling.

He asked me again, "Do you want me to tell you how I know you don't really want God's will?"

"Yes."

I couldn't wait for him to say whatever it was so I could quickly disprove it.

He said, "The reason I can tell that you don't really want God's will is because every sentence you are saying to me starts with the word 'I.' You are in control. God isn't."

I felt like I had been hit in the stomach with a ton of bricks. I could hardly breathe.

All I could do was say, "Wow! I hear you."

We talked briefly. I said "Thank you." Then we said our goodbyes.

CR&SO

I couldn't wait to get off the phone to talk to God about what I had just heard from my brother. Truth is, I thought I was much closer to God than my brother, but I also knew that God had just spoken to me through my brother, Richard. It was a profound statement, and I needed to hear more directly from God about it.

I knew what Richard said to me was absolutely true. Unknowingly, I had been so concerned about what I wanted that God's will hardly mattered. I was in control.

Strangely, I would have argued with anyone—as I had with Richard—if they had suggested that I wanted anything but God's will. But something happened during the few brief moments I spoke with my brother during that December 9 phone call. I got a glimpse into what God had poured supernaturally into my brother. I also realized how little I knew about true spirituality.

C%80

That morning I made a major decision. I wanted to get off the throne of my life. I got on my knees by my breakfast table and asked God to forgive me.

"I didn't realize how in control I was," I prayed through a torrent of tears. "God, please help me! I hear what you were saying through Richard. I do want Your will. Truly! But I see how I've been in control. God, help me to stop trying to control everything. I repent of this. I've been hurting You, even though I didn't know I was doing it."

When the tears stopped flowing, I opened my Bible and started looking up Scriptures about knowing God's will:

The world and its desires pass away, but the man who does the will of God lives forever.—1 John 2:17

I APPEAL to you therefore, brethren, and beg of you in view of [all] the mercies of God, to make a decisive dedication of your bodies [presenting all your members and faculties] as a living sacrifice, holy (devoted, consecrated) and well pleasing to God, which is your reasonable (rational, intelligent) service and spiritual worship. Do not be conformed to this world (this age), [fashioned after and adapted to its external, superficial customs], but be transformed (changed) by the [entire] renewal of your mind [by its new ideals and its new attitude], so that you may prove [for yourselves] what is the good and acceptable and perfect will of God, even the thing which is good and acceptable and perfect [in His sight for you].—Romans 12:1-2 AMP

Trust in the LORD with all your heart and lean not on your own understanding; in all your ways acknowledge him, and he will make your paths straight [or show you His will, my paraphrase].—Proverbs 3:5-6

I delight to do Your will, O my God.—Psalm 40:8

Jesus answered, "My teaching is not my own. It comes from him who sent me. If anyone chooses to do God's will, he will find out whether my teaching comes from God or whether I speak on my own."—John 7:16-17

For my thoughts are not your thoughts, neither are your ways my ways, declares the LORD.—Isaiah 55:8

The more I studied the Bible and spent time in God's presence that day, the more I realized that while I talked a good talk about wanting to do God's will more than anything, my focus had clearly been on myself, and I had unknowingly been in control of my life.

Talking the talk while failing to walk the walk had gotten me in a lot of trouble.

That morning I made a major decision. I wrote this prayer in my journal: "My precious Lord, I've done this before, and I'm doing it again right now. I give You my life again. I don't want to be in control anymore."

In my heart of hearts, I wanted to do God's will more than anything. I felt freer than any time in my life. I was off the throne. I could trust God to help me.

This was a huge step for me. And this revolutionary new "walking the walk" was just beginning.

C33ᵇᴼ

I knew that God had spoken to me through my brother. God was using Richard to teach me something that I had never learned before. I was hearing it for the first time in my spirit.

Don't get me wrong. Many, many times I had said the phrase, "I want God's will in my life." And I believed all these years what I was saying. But the Lord used Richard to shoot an arrow right through a balloon filled with religious piety and hot air.

The self-deception that I had built up over a lifetime was burst in a moment when Richard said, "The reason I can tell that you don't really want God's will is because every sentence you are saying to me starts with the word 'I.' You are in control. God isn't."

I got it. I heard it.

I can remember the sick feeling in my stomach, thinking how deceived I had been, and I felt broken-hearted for hurting God by being in control and not doing His will.

I didn't feel badly toward my brother in any way. He had been used to liberate me from the spiritual deception.

CONVERSATIONS AND REFLECTIONS

During the coming days, note how many of your sentences start with "I." Perhaps you can even reflect on the past day's conversations. What does the percentage of "I" sentences say about who is in control of your life?

_____

_____

_____

_____

To personalize, write out the words to Proverbs 16:3 from the *Amplified Bible,* if you have a copy available. It features a wonderful paraphrase of this verse. If you don't, look up Proverbs 16:3 in your favorite version and then paraphrase it in modern English:

_____

_____

_____

_____

_____

A PRAYER FOR GOD'S WILL

Thank You, God, for the honor and privilege to spend time in Your presence today. I want Your will more than anything. Help me to focus less on myself. I don't want to be in control anymore, so I turn control of my life over to You. I want to be in the center of Your will, so my plans will be established and successful. Lord Jesus, I pray this in Your precious name. Amen.

2

PRAYER AND MEDITATION: December 13, 2003

May my meditation be pleasing to him, as I rejoice in the LORD. — Psalms 104:34

I wish I could tell you that once I faced the fact that all along I had been wanting Patti's will, not God's will, and once I asked God to take control over my life and started recognizing the presence of the "I" word over and over in my life, everything changed, and I never had to face that challenge again. Not so!

It was a major breakthrough for me, but it certainly didn't signal a life of smooth sailing. In many ways, it was God's way of getting my attention in the beginning of what would be eighteen total phone conversations during the coming eight months.

Above all else, I knew that God had spoken to me through Richard. God had used my brother of few words to teach me something that I had never learned before. I was hearing it for the first time in my spirit.

I wanted God to be in control. What I mean by "in control" is not that I wanted him to take away the free will that he gave not just me but all of us. What I wanted, and still want, was for God to help me *surrender* every minute of every day to His will and ways. I wanted to be able to say, "God, Your will be done in every aspect of my life," and mean it. Prior to this time I had been continually saying the right words, but keeping myself off the throne was the ongoing problem.

Richard recognized my battle. In nearly every one of our subsequent conversations, at some point my brother would get tickled. He'd chuckle and say, "You're in control again. You're taking everything back again."

It was an argument that I could not win. He was right. I had spent most of my life on the throne. It would be a life-long battle to get me off and allow God to have first place.

By contrast, Richard seemed totally at peace. It was obvious that he had fought the same battle under quite different circumstances. That's why he would get tickled at me. It was hilarious to him that I kept trying to take over my life again and again. He understood.

At the same time, my life began to change. Inwardly, I knew that this was a big deal. God had come to my rescue. Though I had been through massive struggles before, this time, in many ways, the struggle was worse—it was a constant, discouraging, and humiliating battle against the ongoing rejection and betrayal I felt.

CRAND

The next conversation took place on Saturday, December 13, 2003, four days after Richard's "God's Will, not Patti's Will" phone call.

I am grateful that one of my long-term habits has been keeping a journal. Because of this habit, it was totally natural and instinctive that I not only wrote down what Richard said during each of our conversations, but I also kept a running account of what was going on in my life during that time.

Now, as I look back at the pages surrounding the notes from the December 13 conversation with my brother, my journal is tear soaked. What a painful time!

I prayed and spent time reading my Bible, asking God for answers. I kept trying to seek some kind of relief from my Lord. I thought that after the first phone conversation with Richard on December 9, 2003, I had at least settled that God was on the throne of my life.

As I mentioned before, however, the struggle for control of the throne was (and is!) an ongoing battle.

CRAND

Psalm 18:6 tells us, "In my distress I called to the LORD; I cried to my God for help. From his temple he heard my voice; my cry came before him, into his ears." Verse 9 declares, "He parted the heavens and came down."

In the midst of the ongoing feelings of failure as I kept trying to aright myself in what seemed like a bottomless ocean of despair, God did not swoop down and rescue me bodily. Instead, the telephone rang and my brother Richard's voice was on the line.

He was never wordy. In each of our very special conversations during 2003 and 2004, he would get right to the point.

"What do you think prayer is?"

I told him, "It's conversing with God."

"And what do you think meditation is?" he asked.

I was almost scared to answer him after he had lowered the proverbial boom on me during our first conversation. I was a little gun shy.

I thought for a moment and answered, "That's when I read a Scripture, then I ponder it, and God speaks to me through that Scripture."

I had enough teaching to know the difference between *logos* (the written Word of God) and *rhema* (the revealed Word of God). I couldn't use that language with Richard, because he hadn't traveled in religious circles as I had. He didn't know those words. So I struggled to get the point across.

"When I meditate on a Scripture in the Bible," I continued, "it becomes alive to me."

He said, "Well, what do you think about this?"

I sensed instinctively that something profound was coming.

"Prayer is talking to God," he said simply, "and meditation is listening to God."

So simple, I thought, yet it made so much sense.

I had used paragraphs to try to describe the difference. He captured it in one sentence: "Prayer is talking to God, and meditation is listening to God."

"Patti," he continued, "you need to be quiet and meditate when alone with God."

Then he hit me with another thunderbolt: "And you have to remember, Patti, that God doesn't make deals. You cannot manipulate Him."

I looked at my life. I was always trying to make deals with God. I had apparently spent a lifetime trying to make deals with Him. Even in the midst of the messes I was in, I was still desperately trying to negotiate with God. I would pray more, I would spend more time in the Bible, I would do this or that—and maybe God would see how dedicated I was and work out all my problems.

Guilty!

"God doesn't negotiate," Richard explained.

CB80

I barely had time to think through that concept when my brother suddenly shifted subjects. He said, "Patti, when people give advice, they are stepping over the line. Let me tell you about me. I can only tell others what God has shown me. I don't give advice. I'm not God."

It was all too apparent that I was trying to get my older brother to give me some advice. There were all kinds of wonderful Christians who were offering advice, even when I didn't ask for it.

I knew, more and more, that the decisions I was making were crucial and that I had to hear from God. I couldn't just listen to people. For Richard to offer such wisdom about people who gave advice stepping over the line was almost overwhelming. I got it!

The fact that I was "getting it" made my conversations with Richard even more amazing. Here I was, in the midst of one life-changing crisis after another, and I was listening to the one person with whom I had never had much of a relationship. More astounding, I was listening to someone whom I would have never gone to for Christian counseling. Yet he was being used mightily with such a pure word for me, time after time.

Finally, circling around to the concept of prayer and meditation, he said, "You need to get off the phone and meditate."

There was silence for a moment. Then he continued: "Patti, have you ever just sat with God and not read the Bible or talked? Have you ever just sat with God and been still, in silence?"

"No," I said honestly. "I've never done that."

"Well," he said, "that's what you need to do."

CRØO

"Prayer is talking to God," Richard had said. "Meditation is listening to God."

The simplicity of it zapped me to my core. Unknowingly, I had always confused the two. Mostly, I had chattered away, listing all my needs, wants, hurts and desires, and then I called it prayer. Then I would get up and go about my business—like leaving God sitting there.

After saying goodbye to my brother, I quietly asked God to show me verses to teach me to listen, to meditate on Him, to hear Him. Verse after verse reflected the truth in what I had just heard:

When you are on your beds, search your hearts and be silent.—Psalm 4:4

On my bed I remember you; I think of you through the watches of the night.—Psalms 63:6

May my meditation be pleasing to him, as I rejoice in the LORD.—Psalms 104:34

And after the earthquake a fire, but the Lord was not
in the fire; and after the fire [a sound of gentle still-
ness and] a still, small voice. — 1 Kings 19:12 AMP

And in Psalm 1:1-3, we are given more instructions (and
encouragement) for meditating on God's Word:

Blessed is the man who does not walk in the counsel
of the wicked or stand in the way of sinners or sit
in the seat of mockers. But his delight is in the law
of the LORD, and on his law he meditates day and
night. He is like a tree planted by streams of water,
which yields its fruit in season and whose leaf does
not wither. Whatever he does prospers.

God even directs us to meditate on the words He gives
us in the Bible: "Do not let this Book of the Law depart from
your mouth; meditate on it day and night, so that you may
be careful to do everything written in it. Then you will be
prosperous and successful." — Joshua 1:8

I sat there without saying a word, emptying my mind of
all distractions and listening for God's voice.

As I did, I realized how religious and pious and well-
meaning I had been, but my prayer time had always been
about me, me, me.

I knew I needed to repent, right then and there. All along,
I was being religious and pious, but I had missed the boat

entirely. I had never sat quietly with God—without the Bible, a book, or music before me—never!

Suddenly, I was hit with another thunderbolt—God longed to spend time with me. He created me for loving fellowship. He had wanted us to travel together on a precious pathway, and I had turned prayer into a one-direction monologue.

It's no wonder I couldn't hear Him through my chattering and mentally cluttered life. He wanted to give me hope, peace, faith, love, wisdom, joy and encouragement. I had been content with ritual and routine.

Granted, as I quickly learned, spending time with Him in meditation and quietness required faithfulness, transparency, and vulnerability, and free access to my heart—all sound wonderful and meaningful—but they are infinitely harder to practice than my former religious routine.

My brother, in a much shorter time than I, had learned this concept. His life was filled with a peace and a faith that I had never known. Somehow he knew I needed to hear this, and I was so thankful that he had been open enough to share with me.

I was getting to know God in a deeper way than ever before, as described in John 17:3—"Now this is eternal life: that they may know You, the only true God, and Jesus Christ who You have sent."

Psalm 16:11 became real—"You have made known to me the path of life; you will fill me with joy in your presence, with eternal pleasures at your right hand." I spent time in God's presence daily, enjoying it abundantly, living more and more simply for His presence.

ᏧᏋᎠ

My life quickly began to change. No, the problems didn't vanish; they were just heating up. Still, during those first two phone conversations with Richard, I quickly learned not only how much I wanted to be in control, but also how much I had even tried to control my communication with God.

The first two simple conversations stripped away the wonderful-looking (or so I thought) religious coverings in which I had draped myself.

God, during those first two conversations, allowed two of the massive religious pillars to come crashing to the ground around me. A part of me wanted desperately to gather and glue the crumbled pillars back together. Thank God I had enough sense to realize that He was giving me something very special through my brother's words—something deep and supernatural that I would have never received in the natural.

I also became aware of something even deeper and more important. Because I had grown to love Bible study and prayer, I sometimes even substituted those very important pursuits for fellowship with God.

That might not have made sense to me before the conversations with my brother. Bible study is vital. So is prayer. But these wonderful disciplines do not always mean close fellowship with God. I know, because during much of my adult life I have read the Bible and prayed regularly, yet until I learned what it meant to be silent, take time and listen to my heavenly Father, I was not consistently close to Him. Now I hear Him often.

Fellowship, I increasingly learned, does not consist of rituals, routine or activity. Instead, it is a loving exchange of my heart and life for His love, life and Spirit. That involves listening and being, not just doing!

Jesus says, "But seek (aim at and strive after) first of all His kingdom and His righteousness (His way of doing and being right), and then all these things taken together will be given you besides."—Matthew 6:33 AMP. Although books, teachers, radio and television programs, CDs, DVDs and seminars all have a proper place, God must be the Answer. Seek Him first. Then get ready for wonderful things to be poured out upon your life.

I still have to work at listening and simply spending time in God's presence. I have to remind myself daily of the simple fact that God gave me two ears and only one mouth, and that I need to listen at least twice as much as I talk. It is still a difficult process. After all, I had a lifetime of practice doing it the other way.

And the lessons were just beginning . . .

CONVERSATIONS AND REFLECTIONS

Meditation is often a misused term. In light of Joshua 1:8 and other Scriptures throughout this chapter, what does the Bible say about meditation, and what does this mean for you?

_____

_____

_____

_____

To personalize, write the words to Joshua 1:8 in your own words:

_____

_____

_____

_____

A PRAYER FOR CLOSE FELLOWSHIP WITH GOD

Thank You, God, that You desire fellowship with me. I want fellowship with You, and I long to spend more time every day in Your presence. Help me to spend less time talking and going through the motions. Help me to meditate on Your Word more. Help me to want to be in Your presence. Help me to listen better to You so I can live my life with You and for You. Lord Jesus, I pray this in Your precious name. Amen.

3

TRUST:
January 4, 2004

> Let all those rejoice who put their trust in You; Let
> them ever shout for joy, because You defend them;
> Let those also who love Your name be joyful in
> You. —Psalm 5:11 NKJV

Listening to God speaking to me through Richard took some doing. The initial wariness and prejudice toward my brother came from a lifetime of experience. It also came from decades of trying to do the right thing, going regularly to church, and being what I felt was an upstanding citizen as my mother had modeled.

Richard, by contrast, was an alcoholic, probably from the time he was sixteen or so. I don't remember too much about his drinking, but I do recall that the first time it really hit me how bad it was came during a family Christmas gathering at his house when I was sixteen. Richard was so drunk that he could hardly walk or talk. It was shocking to me because I had never seen him that way before.

As far as I knew, he always cared for his family financially, but he was the true-blue, textbook-definition alcoholic who tried and tried unsuccessfully for years to quit. He was the kind of addict who literally could not take one drink or he was right back into it. I don't know all the places his life took him, but there were many times that our family did not know his whereabouts for days. He would come to and not even know where he had been. And it got worse and worse over the next quarter of a century.

He finally became a Christian after reading Scriptures I had given him during one of his illnesses, including John 3:3—"Jesus declared, 'I tell you the truth, no one can see the kingdom of God unless he is born again.'" He called soon afterward and told me, "I've read the Scriptures you gave me, and your brother is born again!" I can remember being so thrilled!

As I have mentioned before, he tried going to church, but in order to stay free from alcohol, his church became Alcoholics Anonymous. As also previously mentioned, I never thought very much of that. I thought he needed to be in a "real" church.

It wasn't that he minded attending church, but Christians on the whole were too naïve to help him. He was too smart for them, streetwise smart. So smart, in fact, that he could stay addicted for so many years.

"Patti," he told me, "I tried to go to church. I wanted to go to church. But those people couldn't get down where I was and tell me that they knew I was lying, that I couldn't take one drink, I couldn't be around alcohol. They would just say, 'God has healed you. You won't ever deal with this again.' I believed them, then I would go back into it. I think it's wonderful that many Christians are naïve and haven't experienced all the bad things I did, but sometimes they're ill-prepared to reach out to someone like I was. It took someone who went through the gutter like I did to be able to look me in the eye and shoot straight with me, to tell me when I was lying."

Thankfully, God was merciful to Richard, reached down where he was, and lovingly, patiently pulled him out of the alcoholism that held him prisoner for so many years.

I often wondered why my brother and I went on such different paths. We grew up with the same parents, lived in the same small town, and shared friendships with kids from the same neighborhoods. But I eventually discovered that there were things that happened that I didn't know about.

I also developed a new appreciation for what he had learned from God—the supernatural wisdom that poured out from a very human source during each of our special conversations.

CR&O

When I received the third call on Sunday, January 4, 2004, it was very early in the morning, as with most of our conversations. Both of us are early risers, so sometimes we would talk as early as 6 AM. Then after we would talk, I would spend time with God as daylight started to spread over my home and the birds would begin singing so beautifully.

I distinctly remember something else happening after many of our early morning conversations. Off in the distance I would hear a train whistle.

When it happened, that sound would instantly take me back to my childhood in Dexter. The train tracks there went through the center of town, so no matter where you lived, you were close to the sound of the whistle as the locomotives, railroad cars, and caboose rumbled through our village.

By the time the conversations began with Richard, I had already lived for several years in my Dallas suburb, where the train tracks go through the downtown.

It's strange, but sometimes you forget how important certain sounds are to you. The sound of that early morning train whistle would instantly take me back to the comfort and security of my childhood.

Increasingly, that whistle in the distance became such a soothing sound to me after my conversations with Richard. It was like a signal from God. I had never noticed the sound of the train much in my town until those conversations started. Then I would hear the whistle and be reminded of the comfort of growing up in such a safe, secure, protected environment.

CB80

Just before Richard's third call, the New Year of 2004 had been celebrated. While I wanted to be filled with hope and direction, what I wrote in my journal reflected more what I was experiencing, which wasn't good.

Richard sensed it.

"Trust has to be earned," he said, getting right to the point. "You have every right to not trust people."

I waited a moment, letting that thought sink in.

"Other people have to take responsibility for their behavior," Richard continued. "Once trust has been lost and broken, it has to be earned again. Trust has to be earned, whether we like it or not. Until other people face and admit they have a problem and go where they can get help, they can't be helped. You are not responsible for them."

Then Richard turned the spotlight directly on me. "Patti, how responsible do you feel you are for others?"

"I'm not."

"Then get out of the way!"

Then he explained: "What I had to do, as an alcoholic, is I had to choose to associate with the solution, not the problem. I had to choose to associate with people who have walked in the same shoes I had walked in and chose to pursue God in the things I'm sharing with you."

That was it. My brother never was wordy. He spoke very simply, got to the point, and shot an arrow right to the heart of the matter.

CR&O

After our good-bye, I was left to process all that I had heard. As with every conversation I had with my brother, when I got off the phone, I felt I needed to get down on my knees because I was so repentant. I didn't understand everything, but I felt so sorry.

Truthfully, I still didn't know the total picture of what I was sorry about yet. But I knew that God was doing something new in my life. And I knew it was something that I had never learned before. I also knew I had never read such straightforward statements of truth in my studies. Yet I knew it was from God. I was at the bottom and ready to listen.

I began to understand that in my relationships with others, my natural inclination was to think that it was up to me to fix things. I thought I needed to be more forgiving. I thought I needed to help build the bridges between us. I thought I absolutely, positively needed to force myself to be more trusting.

I was wrong. Where in the Bible did God tell me to trust people? It didn't! It was up to others to earn my trust. I could only give trust when it was earned.

What Richard told me made me feel as if a ton of bricks had been taken off of my shoulders.

ॐ

Thankfully, even as I tried to resolve the trust issue with others, I was learning the meaning of Psalm 56:3-4: "When I am afraid, I will trust in you. In God, whose word I praise, in God I trust; I will not be afraid."

No matter what happened, I knew I had to trust in God. He, above all, was trustworthy. Total trust in Him would dispel all fear. Trusting in Him, in fact, signaled a refusal to give into fear. It meant turning to the Lord even during the darkest, bleakest hours.

I knew that He was a good God who wanted to give all of His children good things, so I had to cling to Him, even as Job wrote when he went through his most difficult times— "Though he slay me, yet will I trust Him."—Job 13:15 NKJV

I had to be like the psalmist David, who wrote, "Let all those rejoice who put their trust in You; Let them ever shout for joy, because You defend them; Let those also who love Your name Be joyful in You."—Psalm 5:11 NKJV

Joyful?

Yes. No matter what happens.

CONVERSATIONS AND REFLECTIONS

Do you often feel responsible for others? If so, how? More importantly, how can you get out of the way so God can deal directly with them?

_____

_____

_____

_____

_____

To personalize, write the words to Psalm 56:3-4 in your own words:

_____

_____

_____

_____

A PRAYER OF TRUST

Thank You, God, for being patient with me, despite my faltering trust in You. Now, more than ever, I choose to place my trust in You, no matter what happens. I also choose to place my trust in You for my loved ones and friends. Help me to spend more and more of my time in Your fellowship, learning to trust You deeper than ever before, knowing that as I trust You more, You will pour joy and peace into my life. Amen.

4

ACTION AND DIRECTION: January 23, 2004

Teach me to do Your will, for You are my God; let Your good Spirit lead me into a level country and into the land of uprightness." —Psalm 143:10 AMP

On Friday morning, January 23, I wasn't sure where that "level country" or "land of uprightness" mentioned in Psalm 143 would be. I had been volunteering as the regional administrator of an international women's ministry of which I had been a part for almost thirty years.

Their Chief Executive Officer was retiring, and someone from their headquarters traveled to the Dallas-Fort Worth area to interview me and ask if I would apply for the CEO position.

I was floored, of course, yet honored beyond words. I promised to pray about it. If so led, I would send the requested information.

CR&O

My next conversation with Richard happened three days after my visit with the ministry representative.

My brother was very street smart. He didn't go to college, except to barber school. His English wasn't perfect. But when he said things about himself, I listened, because I knew God was teaching me through him.

I wrote things down exactly as he said them. I am so grateful that God gave me the presence of mind to do so.

"Patti," Richard said as we began our fourth phone conversation, "when I get direction, where I get in trouble is if I don't take action on it. Everything has been presented to me, so I need to take action on it. Then God can do His will, whatever that is."

I wrote as quickly as I could. He seemed to sense that I was doing so, so occasionally he hesitated briefly and then he would continue.

"Taking action is my part," he said after a short pause, "and I leave the outcome to Him."

I finished writing, but didn't want to interfere with what he wanted to say, so I waited for him to talk.

"There is no coincidence with God," he said finally. "Small miracles come from God, and He prefers to remain anonymous. But things don't happen by accident."

Immediately, I thought of this women's ministry opportunity that appeared to be coming my way. I knew that what I was being told by God through Richard was that I had to take action first of all by giving the opportunity to God and saying, "Your will be done! I don't want my will. I don't want their will. I want Your will."

Then the outcome was up to God! It made such sense, though I must admit that I had always been the kind of person who tended to try and *make* things happen. Having the faith to leave the outcome up to God was a new thing for me. The mere fact that I was willing to do so helped me understand that my walk with the Lord had progressed much since my first conversation with Richard. I was not chosen for the CEO position, but it was an honor to be considered.

C3&0

Before we said good-bye, Richard left me with these words: "When you are faced with decisions, pray, 'Dear God, I turn this situation over to You and whatever happens, I know it is Your will.' Then the timetable is up to Him. The results are up to Him. If you have truly turned your life and your will over to God, then you should be peaceful because you are not in control."

I remained quiet as I wrote, and he continued, "Patti, God will give you direction. Problems come when we don't follow the direction He gives us. Taking action is our part. We leave the outcome to Him."

Speaking of himself, he said, "If I have truly turned my life and my will over to God, then life should be relaxing because I'm not in control. When you pray and give a situation to God, remember that you are human and you will try to take it back. That is why you have to stop and say, 'Your will be done!' Say it again and again. Sometimes I've even said it fifty times a day. Then say, `Dear God, I turn this situation over to You and whatever happens, I know it is Your will."

This was a major revelation for me. I had heard many times before about giving *my life* to God, but I had never heard of giving *my will* to Him.

Finally, before we ended this fateful conversation, Richard added for emphasis, "Remember, the timetable is up to God. The results are up to God."

CRED

As usual after our early morning conversations, I watched the sunrise and listened for the distant train whistle.

God then pointed out one of my bigger weaknesses—too often I believed that everyone else was smarter than me. I believed that everyone else knew more than I did. I discounted the wisdom and discernment that God has given me, even to the point that I could ignore the red flags.

I knew that the Bible said much about being aware of what God was doing every day:

> Be imitators of God, therefore, as dearly loved children and live a life of love, just as Christ loved us and gave himself up for us as a fragrant offering and sacrifice to God. . . .Let no one deceive you with empty words, for because of such things God's wrath comes on those who are disobedient. Therefore do not be partners with them. For you were once darkness, but now you are light in the Lord. Live as children of light (for the fruit of the light consists in all goodness, righteousness and truth) and find out what pleases the Lord. Have nothing to do with the fruitless deeds of darkness, but rather expose them. For it is shameful even to mention what the disobedient do in secret. But everything exposed by the light becomes visible, for it is light that makes everything visible… Be very careful, then, how you live—not as unwise but as wise, making the most of every opportunity, because the days are evil. Therefore do not be foolish, but understand what the Lord's will is.—Ephesians 5:1-2, 6-17

Yes, once again I knelt on my knees. My heart had been laid bare before the Lord.

Yes, once again I repented, even though I already sensed that the battle was far from over. I knew myself well enough to realize that through the years when God gave me direction and guidance, I had often tried to help Him along by coming up with slight improvements to His plan—audible chuckle!

Sometimes I would simply question whether I had actually heard from God or not, even when I was absolutely certain at first that I had. It was as if I thought I could wait God out and convince Him to change His plans for my life. Often I obviously felt that I had a better, quicker, more efficient way that would bring the same results.

Wrong!

This time, though, I realized that something different was taking place. God was giving me a new awareness of myself and the people around me. I was still an emotional basket case too many times, and I was still unsure of being able to hear God and follow His instructions.

But something was vastly different. I couldn't explain it, but I could sense it. I only hoped that it was permanent, and that this newfound growth would help me weather the coming storms that I knew I would have to face.

Mainly I knew that something very special was happening. It was as if the last part of the verse in Luke 1:19 (AMP) was especially for me: "I stand in the [very] presence of God, and I have been sent to talk to you and to bring you this good news." It was as if Richard had been sent back with teaching that I needed to hear, and I wanted to hear more!

CONVERSATIONS AND REFLECTIONS

As you learn to say, "Your will be done!" more and more during your conversations with God, what does that statement mean specifically for you?

_____

_____

_____

_____

_____

To personalize, write the words to Psalm 143:10 in your own words:

_____

_____

_____

_____

A PRAYER OF FAITH

Thank You, God, for patiently guiding my life. My problem, too often, is not taking action when You give me direction. Help me to take action when You show me what to do, and help me make the choice to let You do Your will, whatever that is, without my interference. Taking action is my part, and I will leave the outcome to You, for You always know what is best for me. Amen.

5

FREEDOM:
January 24, 2004

Then you will know the truth, and the truth will set
you free. — John 8:32

In between the phone conversations with my brother, I
had a lot of time to reflect on how I had gotten where I
was in 2003 and 2004. Many of the memories filled me with
warmth and hope. Others helped me see that my life had
been a series of similar patterns.

Frankly, when I began having the phone conversations
with Richard during late 2003 and into 2004, I didn't have a
lot of trust in myself and my ability to accurately hear God's
direction.

That feeling, compounded by fear and despair as I went
through the challenges I faced, made each conversation with
my brother even more important and crucial.

CঙৎৎO

On Saturday, January 24, 2004, one day after the "Take Action" conversation, Richard and I talked again early in the morning hours.

Again, I was trying to figure out what I would do in the future, and what was going to happen to me.

Out of the blue, Richard said, "First things first."

"What do you mean?" I asked.

He said, "Don't project into the future. Live only one day at a time. Do what's in front of you today. You do not know what your future holds, but God does. Trust Him."

I listened for more, and then I talked about my hurt, disappointment, and devastation upon learning secrets that had suddenly surfaced in a person I had trusted.

"Everyone has secrets and skeletons in the closet," he continued, "and they have to say, 'I don't want to live this way any more.' That is the only way to true freedom."

CঙৎৎO

Somehow, in God's perfect timing, the seemingly disjointed things my brother said between "Hello" and "Goodbye" that day made perfect sense.

As I spent time with the Lord, I read and reread these Scriptures:

Let all things be done decently and in order.—1 Corinthians 14:40 KJV

But seek first his kingdom and his righteousness, and all these things will be given to you as well. Therefore do not worry about tomorrow, for tomorrow will worry about itself. Each day has enough trouble of its own.—Matthew 6:33-34

The steps of a [good] man are directed and established by the Lord when He delights in his way [and He busies Himself with his every step]. Though he falls, he shall not be utterly cast down, for the Lord grasps his hand in support and upholds him. I have been young and now am old, yet have I not seen the [uncompromisingly] righteous forsaken or their seed begging bread. All day long they are merciful and deal graciously; they lend, and their offspring are blessed. Depart from evil and do good; and you will dwell forever [securely]. For the Lord delights in justice and forsakes not His saints; they are preserved forever, but the offspring of the wicked [in time] shall be cut off. [Then] the [consistently] righteous shall inherit the land and dwell upon it forever.—Psalm 37:23-29 AMP

The eyes of the Lord are toward the [uncompromisingly] righteous and His ears are open to their cry. The face of the Lord is against those who do evil, to cut off the remembrance of them from the earth. When the righteous cry for help, the Lord hears, and delivers them out of all their distress and troubles. The Lord is close to those who are of a broken heart and saves such as are crushed with sorrow for sin and are humbly and thoroughly penitent.—Psalm 34:15-18 AMP

It is better to trust and take refuge in the Lord than to put confidence in man. It is better to trust and take refuge in the Lord than to put confidence in princes.—Psalm 118:8-9 AMP

But as for me, I will look to the Lord and confident in Him I will keep watch; I will wait with hope and expectancy for the God of my salvation; my God will hear me. Rejoice not against me, O my enemy! When I fall, I shall arise; when I sit in darkness, the Lord shall be a light to me.—Micah 7:7-8 AMP

Later, I wrote in my journal:

This time has been given to me to know God in a more intimate way and to learn to completely depend on Him. How wonderful! I'm blessed! God has a purpose for me and He will provide for me here. That is the only way I can gain true freedom from the past — to follow Your guidance and to trust in You.

God had a plan for me. All along He had ordered my life, even when I saw nothing but chaos. Even through the worst of times, God was teaching me and preparing me for what lay ahead. When I understood and accepted it, I felt such a freedom that only God could bring into my life.

CONVERSATIONS AND REFLECTIONS

You have been hurt, disappointed and possibly even devastated by events in your life. Have you been able to say, "I'm not going to let those things in my past control me anymore?" If so, what caused you to say those words? If not, what is holding you back from making that decision?

_____

_____

_____

_____

To personalize, write the words to John 8:32 in your own words:

_____

_____

A PRAYER OF FREEDOM

Thank You, God, for helping me to be free indeed. I am choosing to depend upon You and learning to completely trust You. Help me to follow Your direction and guidance, for that is the only way I can gain true freedom from the past. I believe that You are teaching and preparing me for what happens tomorrow, and I truly seek to understand and accept Your will in everything I do and say. Amen.

6

WHY?
January 25, 2004

Trust in the LORD with all your heart and lean not on your own understanding; in all your ways acknowledge him, and he will make your paths straight.—Proverbs 3:5-6

Conversations with Richard had taken on new meaning for me. The first time, he had called me. Most of the times after that, I called him.

The conversations had also taken on some semblance of regularity—always early in the morning, just before the birds started singing, and before the train whistle moaned through my Dallas suburb.

Increasingly, what led up to each conversation was the fact that I was so hungry to hear more of what God wanted to tell me. I was ready to hear what God planned to give me through the unlikely source of my own brother. I had digested everything from the last conversation and I was ready to hear from God again.

Mostly, the first few conversations were as if God allowed Richard's words to be a pinprick that burst my bubbles of deception and self-righteousness. They got my attention. I no longer put up all the usual defense mechanisms.

I was absorbing the Bible, praying, meditating and spending hours and hours with God. Yet I was learning that when I got on the phone with my brother, God was using Richard to help change my life. By this time I had caught on to the way God was speaking to me through my brother.

CBEO

Richard and I spoke again on Sunday, January 25, 2004. This was highly unusual, because it was the third day in a row that we had a conversation. Usually they were spaced farther apart.

During the brief phone call, apparently I asked my brother questions that had the word "Why?" in them:

"Why is this happening to me again?"

"Why do I have to keep going through this same old song with a different person?"

"Why . . .?"

The gist of it all was that I had had two husbands, yet the same problem. Both had been deceiving me for years. Both were such experts at lying smoothly. Both were husbands that I had loved and trusted. To sum it up, I was left alone and rejected because of a long-term addiction that each of them had hidden from me.

Richard had heard it all before. Suddenly he said something, short and sweet, that changed everything.

"Patti," he started, "I've learned that I don't ever ask why. All I ask is how."

That got my attention.

Then he said, "I ask, 'How am I dealing with this problem? Am I dealing with it honestly? And am I willing to do God's will?'"

I wrote as quickly as I could, making sure to take down each thought carefully.

He continued—"I've found that these things will take care of themselves if I just say to God, 'I can't handle this. This is Your deal. Your will be done.' Then I ask myself, 'How am I dealing with this?' That seems to take care of it."

☙❧

"How?"

Not "Why?"

Sometimes it amazed me how the simplest of lessons I heard from God through Richard's voice were the most life-changing.

"How am I dealing with this?" he had said.

When I got off the phone and began meditating on what I had heard, I thought of the questions I most often asked. I quickly realized that my inquiries always seemed to focus on "Why?"

Then I realized that my "Why?" questions almost always centered on complaints, gripes, feeling sorry for myself, and thinking that I was the only one in the whole wide world going through something.

"Why?" questions always seemed to come down to whining and whimpering that life was picking on me.

"Why?" questions were self-centered.

In a strange way, "Why?" questions were filled with both self-pity and pride at the same time.

I remembered 1 Peter 5:5, which declares, "God opposes the proud but gives grace to the humble."

By focusing on "Why?" questions all the time, I had allowed a false pride to become a major barrier to God's grace and favor.

"How?" questions, by contrast, focused on what God wanted to do in my life. One of the best verses that came to mind was Proverbs 3:5-6: "Trust in the LORD with all your heart and lean not on your own understanding; in all your ways acknowledge him, and he will make your paths straight."

That verse in the Amplified Bible reads this way: "Lean on, trust in, and be confident in the Lord with all your heart and mind and do not rely on your own insight or under-standing. In all your ways know, recognize, and acknowl-edge Him, and He will direct and make straight and plain your paths."

What a difference!

I quickly discovered that when I asked "Why?" I was *"leaning to my own understanding,"* an attitude Proverbs 3:5 warns against. I was back in control and back on the throne again.

When I asked "How?" I was acknowledging Him in all my ways and He would direct my path.

What a change in focus to begin asking, "How am I dealing with this? How am I doing, Lord—according to Your will?"

"How?" implied an inclination to be obedient.

C3ED

Truth is, Richard had latched onto something that I had never grasped before. I knew the Bible better than he did, but I had never learned the application that gave the kind of consistent peace and straight paths that my brother had.

During the next few days I caught myself asking "Why?" so many times. I tried to ask "How?" more and more.

That turnaround then forced me to realize that I had constantly been questioning God, rather than trusting him.

Worse, I had often used the "Why?" questions to raise doubts as to whether God had my best interests at heart.

Sure, I could quote verses such as Jeremiah 29:11-14:

"For I know the plans I have for you," declares the LORD, "plans to prosper you and not to harm you, plans to give you hope and a future. Then you will call upon me and come and pray to me, and I will listen to you. You will seek me and find me when you seek me with all your heart. I will be found by you," declares the LORD, "and will bring you back from captivity."

But did I really trust God to come through with those promises? By constantly whining, "Why?" I questioned God's intentions again and again.

Was I going to let myself be filled with bitterness and resentment, becoming a grudge-bearer, or could I trust Him to walk with me?

Could I believe that He would bring to my mind what He had taught me in the Bible?

And could I behave as a faith-filled, obedient believer, even during suffering?

"How?" is what I worked on until the next conversation with my brother.

CONVERSATIONS AND REFLECTIONS

Our real work in life is growing spiritually and walking out that growth, rather than asking "Why?" In practical terms, how can you begin to grow in faith as you ask "How?" instead of "Why?"—even during challenges and hurts?

_____

_____

_____

_____

_____

To personalize, write the words to Proverbs 3:5-6 in your own words:

_____

_____

_____

_____

PRAYER FOR DIRECTION AND TRUST

Thank You, God, for guiding me, even when I have kept asking "Why?" Help me to learn not to ask that anymore, but to choose to ask "How?" I long to see Your hand at work in my life as I learn to follow Your direction and guidance. I truly seek to understand and accept Your "How?" in everything I do and say. Amen.

7

FEAR:
January 31, 2004

There is no fear in love. But perfect love drives out fear, because fear has to do with punishment. The one who fears is not made perfect in love.—1 John 4:18

The first conversation back on December 9 had knocked me to the floor. I knew then that my brother knew some things that I didn't know. I knew he had received them from God. Each subsequent telephone talk caused more of my foundations to crumble as I realized how my pious thinking had been so off-track.

During one of our early talks he sensed what was going on far below the surface. He told me, "If you want to have these conversations, you'll have to accept the fact that I'll just have to be blunt with you. I'm going to be straightforward. I'm going to tell you how I see it, and you've got to be able to take it."

I said, "I will. I want to hear what you have to say."

Everything he said made such sense to me, so I kept listening.

And in the process, God profoundly changed my life.

C820

I had lots of questions going through my mind. Not only were there lots of challenges, but again and again I remember having such fear about my future and starting all over again.

Thankfully, since I was living alone, I had day after day to spend time with God. I had a lot of time to meditate and a lot of time to read the Bible. And thankfully I had those precious conversations with my brother to help me learn things that I never knew before.

Somehow, God knew the perfect, simple way to talk to me through Richard.

C820

On Saturday, January 31, 2003, when Richard and I had our seventh of these very special conversations, I was at a turning point in my life and I had no idea what my future would hold. Apparently the fear was evident. My brother had talked before at times about fear, but this conversation focused on the subject. Obviously the Lord was giving him words that I needed to hear.

"Don't get in fear," my brother said very simply.

I thought, "That's easier said than done."

Then, as he did so often, rather than offering teaching without application, he began talking about himself: "The only reason I have fear is when I try to run the show. I'm in control. If I'm afraid of the outcome of something, I'm following my own will. I'm not operating in faith."

I wrote as furiously as I could. He waited a moment and then he continued.

"Don't get in fear. Fear of the unknown is normal. Having fear of the results is not normal. We are to leave the results up to God. Fear is a lack of faith. We can't have fear and faith at the same time."

He hesitated. I wasn't sure if he was finished or just giving me more time to write. Finally, he said, "I pay attention to my faith and quit doubting everything. People make themselves miserable by asking the question, `What if?' He said about himself, "A big reason I become fearful is when I try to run the show. If I'm afraid of the outcome of something, I am still following my own will and I'm trying to run the show. I'm not operating in faith."

Then we offered a few pleasantries and said our goodbyes.

CB&C

As I spent time with the Lord afterward, I felt especially led to three passages in Scripture:

For God hath not given us the spirit of fear; but of power, and of love, and of a sound mind. — 2 Timothy 1:7 KJV

The Amplified Bible for that verse renders it this way:

For God did not give us a spirit of timidity (of cowardice, of craven and cringing and fawning fear), but [He has given us a spirit] of power and of love and of calm and well-balanced mind and discipline and self-control.

So do not fear, for I am with you; do not be dismayed, for I am your God. I will strengthen you and help you; I will uphold you with my righteous right hand. For I am the LORD, your God, who takes hold of your right hand and says to you, Do not fear; I will help you. — Isaiah 41:10, 13

In God I trust. I will not be afraid. What can man do to me? — Psalm 56:11

CR80

The more I meditated on what Richard told me, a major realization began breaking through. Fear had been like a hulking giant in my life, always in the shadows, never far from my thoughts. Fear and worry both have tormented me most of my adult life, even as a Christian.

I don't remember being afraid during my childhood, so apparently this was something that had developed more and more after I became an adult. Maybe the seeds of fear were there before, but I don't recall them. I always felt very fulfilled and happy as a young person.

I still don't know exactly when all this fear came upon me. Perhaps it was a gradual process as I dealt with the complexities of adulthood. Regardless of where fear came from and when it all happened, I knew that I had to take responsibility for myself. I had to do it immediately. I was living a divided life between fear and faith. I had counseled others many times about fear, yet I was still living in the middle of fear itself.

When my brother told me I can't have fear and faith at the same time, something clicked. I got it! It was so simple, yet as foundational as a granite bedrock. I remember thinking, I can't have fear and faith at the same time! Wow!

Mark 4:40 (KJV) bears this out—"And he said unto them, 'Why are ye so fearful? How is it that ye have no faith?'"

You cannot have fear and faith at the same time!

"I choose faith," I remember saying. "I refuse fear and worry." I realized that I would have to keep making this choice, but the need to make a decision was never more obvious.

Strangely enough, the more and more I have learned to make this daily (and often hourly) decision, the more I have come to realize that the right choice—faith, not fear—is only possible as I totally surrender and yield my life to God's control.

Again, this seems so simple, yet it goes to the core of humankind's most basic challenge—trusting God and totally surrendering our will to God's will.

During the course of these very special conversations with my brother, the most basic theme, "Your will be done," would be repeated again and again. It always seemed to come back to that point.

And in the process, I can honestly say that life, with all the challenges I would continue to face (and there were many more), became not only endurable, but also wonderful. I became closer to God than at any time in my life. I began to know Him intimately. The peace that began flooding my heart was absolutely pure and meaningful.

I had already been walking with God for decades. Before, however, I always seemed to want to build my own road. The results were incredibly evident, extremely painful, and enormously costly. Now, I could start to see that He was straightening my path as I learned to walk in obedience to Him.

MY CONVERSATIONS AND REFLECTIONS

Have you tended to build your own road as you traveled on life's journey, rather than allowing God to do it? If so, what part did fear play in it? In practical terms, how can you choose a deeper faith in God's ability?

_____

_____

_____

_____

_____

_____

To personalize, write the words to 2 Timothy 1:7 in your own words:

_____

_____

_____

_____

PRAYER FOR COURAGE

Thank You, God, for guiding me, even when I have been fearful of the road ahead. Help me to know You intimately, knowing that perfect love in You casts out fear. Straighten my path as I learn how to walk without fear. I seek to understand and accept Your way in everything I do and say. And

I ask you to flood my heart with peace as I follow You more closely. Amen.

8

MEDDLING:
February 3, 2004

In the morning, O LORD, you hear my voice; in the
morning I lay my requests before you and wait in
expectation. — Psalm 5:3

My next conversation with Richard was early on
Thursday, February 3, 2004. It began very simply
when he said, "We will always tend to meddle in God's business, but catching ourselves when we start to do it is what's
important."

He waited for me to really hear what he was saying: "You
can't control people, places or things. Do you know why?"

I said, "No," simply because I couldn't wait to hear what
he was going to say next!

He continued, "Because you do not have that power.
Pray for people. Give them to God, then say, 'Your will be

done.' The outcome is God's. The timing is His. The results are His."

CଔଔO

After saying good-bye in the still-early morning hours, I watched the sunrise through the trees, listened to the distant train whistle, and meditated on what I had heard from my brother.

It was inarguable. I had been trying to control people, places and things all my life. I'm not sure I had realized how ingrained it was in me!

Richard was right. I hated to admit it, but it is true that I don't have power to change people, places, things, timing or the outcome. If I am honest in my prayer, "Your will be done," then the outcome is God's. Not mine!

It was so obvious, once I received this truth. I couldn't change people, places or things. God could, but I couldn't.

Lots of things were impossible with me, no matter how hard I tried, yet "Nothing is impossible with God" (Luke 1:37). What a difference accepting that fact would make in my life.

What I was beginning to learn by this time, for the very first time in my thirty-five years as a Christian, was how to *wait* upon God. It was about time! God was teaching me, through my brother, how to wait on Him, and I was finally getting it!

It wasn't an easy lesson to learn. During that time, I felt like I was being pressured to make some major life-changing decisions.

It wasn't just the fact that it felt like a pressure cooker, but it was the idea that it felt like someone kept turning up the heat. And it was so tempting to just make a decision, any decision, to turn down the heat and take the pressure off.

Through my brother, God saw fit to encourage me to learn how to wait.

CR&O

All of my life I have been a doer. I have always been an achiever, competitive, wanting to win at anything I did.

At this time in my life, God was teaching me not to do one thing until He gave direction, and to wait on Him patiently until He did direct me.

Right before this conversation, according to my journal entries, I was trying to wrestle with trying to remember the reality of all that had taken place and where God was in everything that had happened.

I wrote, "I am having a real hard time today, because it would be so easy to just go ahead with the things people are pressuring me to do and put up with whatever happens."

The pressure was on. The temptation to make a snap decision "for the good" was real. Yet because I have always been such a doer, not making a quick decision under pressure was definitely a new walk for me—to do nothing!

Nothing!

I was being led to just spend time with God, stay in His presence and know that He would take care of the situation.

It was as if He was telling me, "You say you want My perfect will in your life? Well, get out of the way and let Me do it!"

I had never quite been at this place before. I was a solutions-type person. I wanted to work things out. That was me—to start going through the details of getting done what needed to be done. But God would not let me.

During our February 3 conversation, Richard said, "We will always tend to meddle in God's business, but catching ourselves when we start to do it is what's important."

CB&O

Over the next few days, I caught myself trying to take over, trying to work out one of my bright ideas, wanting to just do something so I would feel better about the situation.

God kept teaching me to not do anything until He led me to do so.

So I did nothing except spend time with Him. Doing nothing was hard to do.

I was led to go through Scriptures on waiting:

In the morning, O LORD, you hear my voice; in the morning I lay my requests before you and wait in expectation. — Psalm 5:3

We wait in hope for the LORD; he is our help and our shield. — Psalm 33:20

Wait for the LORD and keep his way. He will exalt you to inherit the land; when the wicked are cut off, you will see it. — Psalm 37:34

I wait for you, O LORD; you will answer, O Lord my God. — Psalm 38:15

But those who hope in the LORD will renew their strength. They will soar on wings like eagles; they will run and not grow weary, they will walk and not be faint. — Isaiah 40:31

I would meditate on these verses over and over. Reading and rereading each word. It wasn't as if I didn't know these verses existed. I had read them all before. I just hadn't realized the directions in them were so clear-cut. Like many people, I always thought that the Bible was a lot of suggested guidelines, something like a smorgasbord. I could pick this one or that. I could gloss over those things that I didn't really want to do.

I discovered that the Hebrew word for *wait* means "to wait with hopeful expectancy." That requires trust and humility. It also implies an unlimited confidence.

Waiting on God means putting aside our agendas. By definition, it centers on resting in God.

I mention the need for humility in waiting, as 1 Peter 1:6-7 tells us:

In this you greatly rejoice, though now for a little while you may have had to suffer grief in all kinds of trials. These have come so that your faith—of greater worth than gold, which perishes even though refined by fire—may be proved genuine and may result in praise, glory and honor when Jesus Christ is revealed.

The problem is that we really don't want to go through God's refining fire. I freely admit it!

Yet if we are willing to go through His refining process, then we can come forth as "greater worth than gold," and God will be exalted.

It is just that God's timing is not always the timing we prefer, impatient as we tend to be. We want it now, not later!

But if God has promised you something, you can be sure you will have it. God is faithful to fulfill every promise He gives us and to work things out for good. There may be a waiting period, but it will come to pass. He is not like so many people who make promises but have short memories.

ය්ණ

With something as simple as meddling in God's business, I realized that I had to wait until I heard a word of direction from the Lord, then I could move.

Again, this might be second nature to some people, but it wasn't to me. I always had to make things happen. When I was a youngster who wanted to play the piano, I did whatever it took to learn the lessons. When I wanted to perform as a twirler during high school football games, I did whatever was required (and more) to be the best I could be. When I decided to build my own businesses, nothing was too difficult or time-consuming to keep me from making it work.

I have been in high places. I did build two very successful businesses. I traveled all over the country doing so, and others have shown me much respect in the corporate world. I served on advisory boards and was honored to be president and chaplain of one international association, International Christian Photographers.

I say all that to let you know that I am not downplaying hard work, persistence, or professionalism. All those are admirable qualities. They were right for that time in my life, and they may be wonderful characteristics to use in the future. But during the time of my special conversations with

Richard, I was going through a new era, a different season. God was calling me to do what seemed impossible.

Learning to wait and shift the responsibility of the outcome to God, where it belonged all along, was very difficult.

ᚮᚱᚮ

Ecclesiastes 3 includes a popular passage that has been quoted often in songs, poems and films:

There is a time for everything,
and a season for every activity under heaven:
a time to be born and a time to die,
a time to plant and a time to uproot,
a time to kill and a time to heal,
a time to tear down and a time to build,
a time to weep and a time to laugh,
a time to mourn and a time to dance,
a time to scatter stones and a time to gather them,
a time to embrace and a time to refrain,
a time to search and a time to give up,
a time to keep and a time to throw away,
a time to tear and a time to mend,
a time to be silent and a time to speak,
a time to love and a time to hate.
—Ecclesiastes 3:1-8

To everything there is a season. There is a time for action, but God also often calls us to wait.

How do you know the difference?

I was learning that only when I was in the center of His will—no matter what was going on around me, even when the storms came—only then did I have God's peace in my heart, that "peace of God, which transcends all understanding" that will "guard your hearts and your minds in Christ Jesus."—Philippians 4:7

C3ᎯᎶ

In the process of meditating on God's word concerning the subject of waiting, there was one verse that I had apparently rushed past many times. The truth I read, when I really *read* the verse, was startling:

And let the peace (soul harmony which comes) from Christ rule (act as umpire continually) in your hearts [deciding and settling with finality all questions that arise in your minds, in that peaceful state] to which as [members of Christ's] one body you were also called [to live]. And be thankful (appreciative), [giving praise to God always].—Colossians 3:15 AMP

How does peace from Christ act as an umpire in our hearts?

I have loved baseball since the days when I enjoyed the game as a youngster on my hometown's sandlots and playgrounds. I have enjoyed going to Texas Rangers games through the years I've lived in the Lone Star State. My grandsons have been very good baseball players, and I have sat on many hard wooden and aluminum benches while watching them play. There is something so basic and All-American about the game of baseball.

When I read Colossians 3:15 and focused on what it meant, letting Christ's peace rule as my umpire wasn't a major league jump.

It was no accident that the verse came alive to me during this time. The truth in that verse was like a seed that germinated in my heart and grew rapidly.

The umpire says it. You do it. It is that simple.

I got it. When I don't have peace, I don't. When I have a doubt, I don't. Quite simply, it works. "I don't" means "I don't do what I'm about to do." Make sense?

CONVERSATIONS AND REFLECTIONS

In practical terms, how are you learning to understand the invaluable lesson of waiting on God and His peace, rather than jumping ahead of God's plan for your life?

_____

_____

_____

_____

_____

_____

To personalize, write the words to Psalm 5:3 in your own words:

_____

_____

_____

_____

PRAYER FOR PEACE

Thank You, God, for being with me and helping me along, even when I have been impatient. I know that Your timing is not always my timing. Help me to know the difference, and help me to choose Your direction and timing in everything I do. Thank You for the peace You have promised, and I ask you to flood my heart with peace as I follow you in obedience and faith. Amen.

9

FENCES AND FOUR WORDS: February 4, 2004

Our Father in heaven, hallowed be your name, your kingdom come, your will be done on earth as it is in heaven. Give us today our daily bread. Forgive us our debts, as we also have forgiven our debtors. And lead us not into temptation, but deliver us from the evil one. For if you forgive men when they sin against you, your heavenly Father will also forgive you. But if you do not forgive men their sins, your Father will not forgive your sins. —Matthew 6:9-15

As mentioned previously, I grew up in church, yet I did not become a born again Christian until 1969. I had always been a good person, at least in my eyes. I had worked hard, tried to do right, and thought I was a model citizen. What was there for God not to like?

During the '60s, I was surrounded by others who didn't seem to have any problem with "doing your own thing," as the trendy phrase went.

By this time, I had worked for a large corporation and began looking at the people around me who were the most popular and had it together. They were very different from the way I was brought up. It was no secret that many were sleeping around and doing whatever they wanted, yet they seemed happy.

"Why am I the only one being good?" I finally said. "Everyone else does what they want to do."

In the '60s a popular song's lyrics talked about disappointments in life, suggesting that we do what feels good and have a ball, if that's all there is.

Today, it is depressing to even think about those lyrics. Back then, however, they represented where a lot of people were. It was true, in many ways, for me.

For a short while, I decided to follow this philosophy. I did what I wanted. Oh, I was still a good person and hard worker—I thought, but I did things that I knew I wasn't supposed to do.

It was the '60s, right? Everybody's doing what they want to do, so I thought, "Why not me?"

Unfortunately, doing whatever I wanted to do filled me with guilt and shame. Plus, I hurt others and myself. I was more unhappy than ever.

CR80

Not long after I moved to Fort Worth, I met a young woman named Connie on the train between Fort Worth and Little Rock. Occasionally, I would ride back and forth to visit my family, and the trip included a stop-off in Little Rock on the way to Missouri.

She also lived in Fort Worth at the time, but had grown up in Little Rock. We met quite by accident and started talking. After that she became one of my dearest friends. We would get together occasionally in Fort Worth to catch up on everything going on in our lives, and we also periodically rode the train together to visit our respective homes.

Not only was she a great friend, but she was unabashedly a Christian. So after I "did my own thing" a short while and was left with such horrible feelings inside, I called Connie and asked if I could come to her house to talk.

As we sat at her kitchen table, I began bawling and told her everything.

She said, "Patti, I really think you need to go talk to my pastor."

I had reached the place that I didn't go to church anymore. "Would you be willing to go talk to him?"

"I think I would," I said. "It might make me feel a little better going to talk to him."

She went to the phone and set up an appointment. Within a couple of days we met with her pastor at North Fort Worth Baptist Church.

He asked, "Why are you here?"

That's about all it took for me to start sobbing. I told him what I had done. I felt like a piece of dirt.

The lowest of low.

Horrible!

Finally when I stopped crying so much, he asked, "Okay, Patti, I want to ask you this. Are you a Christian?"

I sobbed, "Yes."

"Well," he asked, "would you like to tell me about the time you became a Christian?"

Even with tears running down my face, I thought that was about the dumbest thing he could ask. Without thinking, I retorted with something even dumber.

"Well," I answered, "I was raised in church, and I live in the United States of America."

That had to be a pretty big giveaway to the pastor that I had no clue what it meant to become a Christian.

Then he started telling me something that I had never heard before. I had grown up in church hearing about God and about Jesus. I believed in God. I celebrated the birth of Jesus every Christmas, and I rejoiced at His resurrection every Easter.

But this pastor told me that God loved me, that He sent His only Son to die for me: "For God so loved the world that he gave his one and only Son, that whoever believes in him shall not perish but have eternal life."

I had learned John 3:16 in my childhood years. All the kids—Methodist, Baptist or whatever—had gone from one vacation Bible school to another in my hometown, so there is no telling how many times I had heard that verse. Like most VBSers, I had made and painted plaques and sung songs about John 3:16.

Sitting in the chair in the pastor's office, I didn't have to be told what sin was. I knew I was a sinner. Yet the pastor told me that God loved me so much that He sent His Son to die for me—"But God demonstrates his own love for us in this: While we were still sinners, Christ died for us" (Romans 5:8). He said that Jesus knew my name when He was dying on the cross, and even as He was dying, He knew all the sins I would commit, even what I had just described. Still, Jesus was willing to die on the cross for me and take every sin upon Him so I could have eternal life.

He reminded me that Jesus died, then rose again miraculously on the third day, was seen by many for a short while, then ascended into heaven and was alive today.

Then the pastor told me about God's plan for me to accept His Son as my Savior and Lord. This meant that I would give Him my life and control over it.

He shared verses such as Romans 6:23—"For the wages of sin is death, but the gift of God is eternal life in Christ Jesus our Lord" and Romans 10:9—"If you confess with your mouth, 'Jesus is Lord,' and believe in your heart that God raised him from the dead, you will be saved."

The pastor told me that because of Jesus' death on my behalf, all I had to do was believe in Him, trusting His death as the payment for my sins, and I would be saved from eternal death and punishment.

I learned that salvation and the forgiveness of sins is available to anyone who will trust in Jesus Christ as their Lord and Savior—"Yet to all who received him, to those who believed in his name, he gave the right to become children of God"—John 1:12.

Best of all, I could have a fresh start, a new beginning, regardless of what I had done in the past—"Therefore, if anyone is in Christ, he is a new creation; the old has gone, the new has come!"—2 Corinthians 5:17.

What a wonderful message was revealed in Romans 5:1, "Therefore, since we have been justified through faith, we have peace with God through our Lord Jesus Christ." That was an amazing thought that through Jesus Christ we can have a relationship of peace with God. I had absolutely no peace inside. That's what I wanted.

At the state I was in, I had no problem understanding what the pastor said and eventually praying to ask Jesus Christ to take away my sins and set me free from my past. When you are in a pit, any direction is up.

And when I prayed to ask Jesus to take over my life, it was as if the pastor and my friend weren't even in the room. I poured my heart out to God.

ᎦᎯᎣ

I walked into the pastor's office that day feeling as if I had a ton of bricks on my shoulders and felt like an old woman, even though I was only twenty-six years old at the time. An hour later, after I confessed my sin to the Lord Jesus and accepted Him into my heart, I knew as I walked out of the pastor's office that something had happened to me.

I felt loved!

Those moments are as real today as they were then. I remember hearing the birds singing as if I were hearing their songs for the first time in a long time.

All of a sudden, it was as if the world around me had turned from black and white into Technicolor®.

My shoulders felt no burdensome weight. I had been born again, as John 3:3 (KJV)declares: "Jesus answered and said unto him, Verily, verily, I say unto thee, Except a man be born again, he cannot see the kingdom of God."

Everything was different!

As the days progressed, I knew that something had happened. I might have looked the same on the outside to others, but I knew something had changed on the inside.

What was different was that I had a love for people that I had never experienced before. To be honest, even before becoming a Christian, while I appeared to be a good person and seemed warm and friendly to others, in my heart of hearts I was mostly concerned about me. I wanted to be happy. I wanted to be popular. I wanted to be well liked. I wanted to reach my goals.

The sudden change went a lot deeper than anything I could have imagined. I found myself walking through the grocery store and seeing some woman wheeling her cart through the aisles, wondering, "Does she know how much God loves her?"

I would drive past another motorist and ask, "Does he know that Jesus died for him?"

I wanted to run up to people and share what had happened to me. I wanted loved ones and friends to have what I had. I had a newfound love for people.

CB80

By 2003 and 2004, during the conversations with my brother, I had been an active Christian for nearly thirty-five years, reading all the right books, watching the popular Christian TV programs, and receiving the best, life-changing teachings.

I had lots of religious language, dogma and behavior, but as I learned more about myself, I was shocked to realize how little faith I really had.

My friends, fellow churchgoers, and even my business associates thought I was a mature Christian. They would come to me for prayer. They would come to me for advice.

But my life was changing during our phone conversations. God kept showing me that He was causing the change.

Like the Prodigal Son's older brother in the Bible, I had pretty much been the good child, and now I was hearing this simple yet profound wisdom from a guy who had spent most of his lifetime away from God and in a daily struggle even after he became a Christian to overcome a terrible bondage to alcohol.

It was a bit disconcerting, yet these words of wisdom coming from Richard had even more authenticity because he was such an unexpected source.

During these conversations, I discovered what little true faith I really had. I had been spiritually deceived. I had built up religious-looking walls that were human, not spiritual.

"Perception is reality," the old saying goes. It was certainly true for me. My false perceptions had become very real to me. I thought I was full of faith. Others thought I was full of faith. But I was full of fear, worry and false pride, and Richard's phone calls burst bubble after bubble of deception.

Thankfully, I chose to listen. More importantly, I chose to receive what God was telling me through my brother.

Cʒꙮꙅꙩ

I had several major decisions to make, and the necessity to make those choices would not go away.

On Wednesday, February 4, the early morning phone call with my brother started on an interesting note.

I told him about the choices I was facing.

"Before you move a fence," Richard said, "always find out the original reason it was put there in the first place."

What?

I tried to understand what he was saying. Before I make a major change, I needed to consider why I made the original decision in the first place?

In other words, why was that fence put there? Maybe it needed to be moved or removed, but it was worth going back to determine why it was built there.

Since that time, the "fences" principle has given me reassurance and helped me many times when I would have made a choice without thoroughly thinking it through.

But at that time, I didn't have much time to think about Richard's statement. I had barely written down the first statement when he began another thought.

Cʒꙮꙅꙩ

During many of the conversations, no matter how hard I tried to hide it, I'm sure my thoughts and fretting were broadcast loud and clear.

Several times my brother would chuckle and say, "You're trying to be in control again!"

During this conversation, he offered more insight and practical application on the subject that was definitely an Achilles' heel for me (and probably most Christians!).

He said, "There are four important words you need to be praying, and sometimes you might have to say these words fifty times a day."

I was thinking, "Only four words?"

"What are they?" I asked.

"Here they are," he said. "Thy will be done."

I wanted something a bit more substantial, but I kept writing as my brother kept teaching.

"First," he continued, "you have to turn your life and your will over to God. When you pray, you then have to accept the outcome. You are a human being. Worry, fear and trying to control will come back on you and you will try to interfere. When this happens, stop and say again, 'Thy Will Be Done.' Your own will tells you that you are weak if you give up. The reality is that you are surrendering to a power greater than you, and that's what God wants."

He stopped for a moment as I wrote hastily, wanting to capture each word.

"Patti," he urged, "you are going to have to quit trying to run your own life. Pray 'Dear God, take all of me. I am yours to do with as you see fit.' Then see what happens."

I listened intently, waiting for what would come next.

"It's no different with me," he said. "Every day I need to honestly and sincerely turn my life and my will over to God and say, 'Thy will be done.' Sometimes I have to say it fifty times a day!"

He had mentioned this before, but as he shared on this Wednesday morning, I again began to realize how much I had been in control of my life as a Christian, and how much I kept trying to take back the throne of my life. It sickened me.

ଔଞ୍ଚ

I got off the phone and repented again. I asked for forgiveness for still running my own life. I surrendered not only my life, but also my will to my Heavenly Father, again. I realized more than ever that I needed to do this daily!

"Thy will be done!"

I said the phrase over and over during the coming days. I cannot get along without praying these four words anymore. Every time I would start getting frustrated, confused, aggravated, resentful, irritated, or fearful, I knew that I was trying to be in control again.

Jesus clearly explains the abundant life in John 10:10 AMP—"The thief comes only in order to steal and kill and destroy. I came that they may have and enjoy life, and have it in abundance (to the full, till it overflows)."

What I've learned is that the abundant life takes a very simple acceptance of God's will, no matter what happens. I know I must continue to pray, *"Not my will but Thy will be done."* It may not turn out the way I want, but it will be the best way in the long run, because it is God's way.

I have also learned that happiness isn't something you try to find. Doing God's will brings true happiness.

☙❧

Just as I had to make a decision whether or not to listen and accept what was given to me by God in the conversations with my brother, I also had to make a conscious and continual decision to accept that whatever results is God's will for me.

Each time I make that choice, my burdens become so much lighter:

Come to me, all you who are weary and burdened, and I will give you rest. Take my yoke upon you and learn from me, for I am gentle and humble in heart, and you will find rest for your souls. For my yoke is easy and my burden is light.—Matthew 11:28-30

That is why I have learned to pray—again and again—the prayer provided at the end of this chapter. Perhaps it will help you, too.

CONVERSATIONS AND REFLECTIONS

The abundant life takes a very simple acceptance of God's will, no matter what happens. It may not turn out the way you want, but it will be the best way in the long run, because it is God's way. In practical terms, how can you increasingly pray *"Not my will but Thy will be done,"* and how do you think it will affect your life?

_____

_____

_____

_____

To personalize, write the words to John 10:10 in your own words:

_____

_____

_____

_____

PRAYER FOR CONTENTMENT WITH GOD'S WILL

Dear Lord, I give You my life and my will today. May Your will be done. I trust You, God, to answer my prayers as You see fit. I ask You to give me Your grace and mercy to be content with Your will for me. Please help me get out of Your way. Amen.

PRAYER TO BECOME A CHRISTIAN

Dear God, I repent of my sins. I ask You to forgive me. Lord Jesus, I ask You to come into my heart and be my Lord and Savior. Amen.

10

THE ELEVENTH COMMANDMENT: February 10, 2004

I press on toward the goal to win the prize for which God has called me heavenward in Christ Jesus.— Philippians 3:14

This Tuesday morning telephone call covered several things, but with one major focus.

I was explaining several things going on:

"I guess I shouldn't have done . . ."

"Maybe I should have done . . ."

I sometimes felt like the worst failure on earth.

Finally Richard said, "There should be an eleventh commandment."

"Really?" I said. "What should it be?"

"Thou shalt not 'should' on yourself."

"What do you mean?" I asked.

"Well," he continued, "people say, 'I shoulda done this' or 'I shoulda done that.' That isn't faith, Patti. That is fear."

After a moment of silence he continued. "Fear is a lack of faith. Pay attention to your faith."

In all the years before the special phone calls with Richard, he had never used phrases like this before. I was amazed at how clearly and succinctly he could express things.

"The only reason I have fear is when I try to run the show," he concluded. "If I'm afraid of the outcome of something, I'm following my own will. I'm not operating in faith."

And then he added, "'Shoulds' keep you from going forward."

End of conversation.

Cₒₑₒₐₒ

Each time after we said goodbye, I'd get off the phone and either get on my knees and repent or start reading my journal notes. It was like reading something from another world, even though it was very down to earth.

How many times had I heard and confessed the words from 2 Timothy 1:7 (KJV)—"For God hath not given us the spirit of fear; but of power, and of love, and of a sound mind." Still, I never heard until these conversations with my brother that when I have fear, it's because I'm trying to run the show of my life. Nor had I thought of the fact that being afraid of the outcome means that I am following my own will, not living in faith.

I had been saying all the right things for years, confessing the Bible Scriptures, yet I was fearing the outcome of things.

Even though I was learning to wait on God, I still wanted to fix everything and be active, but God was helping me to wait. Waiting on God and not fearing the outcome continued to be a radical departure from my past.

I realized, more than ever, that I wanted to keep going forward in life, not backward.

"Don't 'should' on yourself."

What a powerful statement.

I got off the phone and asked God to help me to never "should" on myself again. I forgave myself, even as Christ had already forgiven me. I gave all the shame, condemnation, guilt and regret to God that day for my entire life.

And I have discovered, again and again, that the hardest person to forgive seems to be myself!

I was also a perfectionist. I now believe that the root of my perfectionism was pride. There is a difference between wanting to do things with excellence for God's glory and wanting to be perfect for my own glory.

James 4:6 tells us, "But he gives us more grace. That is why Scripture says: 'God opposes the proud but gives grace to the humble.'" And Proverbs 16:18 cuts right to the quick: "Pride goes before destruction, a haughty spirit before a fall."

Obviously I still had much to learn!

ఴఏ

God revealed to me something a few days later. I wrote and highlighted it in my journal: "Patti, just be in My presence. I will make things happen the way they are supposed to."

I was having to trust God as never before. I was having to wait on Him as never before. I had to believe that He was really real, and that He was truly concerned about my life—both small and large details.

I had to believe, all or nothing, that He had a plan and a hope for my future.

My faith was on the line. I knew at any time, any day, I could have chucked it all, but I also knew that there was no turning back. I was in new territory.

No, I could not go back. I had to trust God for the outcome. And as I trusted Him, He began showing me how I had tormented myself for years and years. All my life I had been a perfectionist. As simple as it sounds when I put it on paper, it took me a long time to learn that only One who has ever walked on this earth was perfect, and His name is Jesus.

Meanwhile, I had kept setting myself up for failure because I could never measure up.

God showed me that I had to stop being a perfectionist. Still, during the conversations, I began seeing again that I still tended back toward perfectionism. That's why I kept beating myself up with the "shoulds."

I would catch myself thinking, "Why didn't I see this earlier?" Or "I should have done this." I questioned why I hadn't picked up on things better.

I was awfully good at mentally abusing my own self, at "shoulding" on myself.

Once again I started catching myself doing all the "shoulds." I would say, "Okay, this is not something that God wants me to do. All the 'shoulds' have nothing to do with trust and faith. I'm just beating myself up. I can't do it any longer. I've tried to do my best. I've failed miserably at times. I'm a sinner. I've repented. All these ups and downs are part of the tapestry of my life. There is no reason for me to keep tormenting myself with all the 'shoulds.' I have to move on."

When Richard hit me with the fact that living in the 'shoulds' is not faith, that it is fear, it was exactly what I needed to hear at that moment in my life.

And even as I strove to learn all that I could, I had a sense of urgency to get all that God wanted to give me through these precious, life-changing conversations with Richard.

MY CONVERSATIONS AND REFLECTIONS

My brother said, "'Shoulds' keep you from going forward." What are some of the "shoulds" that you have used recently, and how are these motivated by fear, not faith? How can you turn those "shoulds" around?

_____

_____

_____

_____

_____

To personalize, write the words to Philippians 3:14 in your own words:

_____

_____

_____

_____

PRAYER FOR FORWARD-LOOKING FAITH

Dear Lord, help me to get rid of the "shoulds" in my life. Help me to stop living in fear as You develop a forward-looking faith in me. I give You my life and my will today. I'm tired of trying to run my own show. May Your will be done. I want Your plan, not mine! Please help me get out of Your way and go forward. Amen

11

1DAAT
February 18, 2004

Therefore do not worry about tomorrow, for tomorrow
will worry about itself. Each day has enough trouble
of its own. — Matthew 6:34

For over thirty years Richard had "1DAAT" on his
Missouri license plates, a positive confession that he
learned to make long before he and God finally overcame his
alcohol addiction. People all over the area knew him because
of those distinctive plates.

1DAAT stands for "One Day at a Time," the AA slogan
that later became a legendary country and Gospel song written
by Marijohn Wilkin and Kris Kristofferson. Remember those
simple, powerful words?

One day at a time, sweet Jesus
That's all I'm asking from You
Just give me the strength to do ev'ryday
What I have to do
Yesterday's gone, sweet Jesus
And tomorrow may never be mine
Lord help me today show me the way
One day at a time.*

I can't tell you how many times I heard that song on the radio—and often sang the lyrics of the song—without grasping the true meaning of the words.

And that 1DAAT theme came through loud and clear during the next phone call with Richard on Wednesday, February 18.

໓ສ

I had written in my journal about the situation I was in:

"I woke up this morning and got in fear as to whether I'm doing the right thing in filing for divorce. Fear came in. I only want to do God's will, but I am afraid that I might mess up. Well, I can't file today, anyway. I've got a full day speaking at a Christian women's

---

* One Day at a Time," written by Marijohn Wilkin and Kris Kristofferson. Used by permission from Buckhorn Music, Nashville.

club and other obligations. I have a guest coming this afternoon. Still, I find myself bringing into today a fear of something that I might be led to do on another day, and it is causing me to worry, even though I can't even do anything about it today."

The apprehension about my future was sometimes overwhelming, even as I was learning so much about my walk with the Lord.

"I find when I try to bring into today what I might do tomorrow it causes me to fear," my brother said over the phone. "We've got to live one day at a time."

I hoped he would say more.

"Don't get in fear," he continued. "I find that when I try to bring into today what I might do tomorrow, it causes me to fear."

Zing!

The arrow went right into my heart.

That described what I often did. I had done it all my life. That's the way I had lived.

Years ago, even after I became a born again Christian, I used to live in a fantasy world. I was always making decisions based on fantasies that I had. I could spiritualize some of the dreams and call them the desires of my heart. God does want to give us the desires of our hearts when He has put those desires there. Still, we have to be wise and prudent with what God has placed in our hands and hearts today.

At the same time, I was a professional at worrying about tomorrow, even though I knew it was beyond my immediate control.

In Matthew 6:34 Jesus tells us, "Therefore do not worry about tomorrow, for tomorrow will worry about itself. Each day has enough trouble of its own." Fear about what might happen or what might not happen tomorrow is not a mindset from God. Yet for some of us it is a natural tendency, and I readily admitted, I was one of those people.

ভাৰ

When I started concentrating on what "living one day at a time" meant, I began to realize that there are two days in every week that I shouldn't worry about: Yesterday and Tomorrow.

Yesterday has passed forever beyond my control. All the money in the world cannot bring back yesterday. I can't erase a single thing I said or did. If yesterday held mistakes, blunders, faults, aches and pains, it has all passed by forever and is totally beyond my control. Yet it's human nature to be bound up in regrets about the past.

The passage in 1 John 1:9 has the 1DAAT answer: "If we confess our sins, he is faithful and just and will forgive us our sins and purify us from all unrighteousness."

Thankfully, when I ask God to forgive me, He also forgets. He even tells us, "Their sins and lawless acts I will remember no more" (Hebrews 10:17).

There are more wonderful passages throughout the Bible that are filled with 1DAAT truths:

Praise the LORD, O my soul, and forget not all his benefits—who forgives all your sins and heals all your diseases, who redeems your life from the pit and crowns you with love and compassion, who satisfies your desires with good things so that your youth is renewed like the eagle's.—Psalm 103:2-5

The Lord is merciful and gracious, slow to anger and plenteous in mercy and loving-kindness. He will not always chide or be contending, neither will He keep His anger forever or hold a grudge. He has not dealt with us after our sins nor rewarded us according to our iniquities. For as the heavens are high above the earth, so great are His mercy and loving-kindness toward those who reverently and worshipfully fear Him. As far as the east is from the west, so far has He removed our transgressions from us. As a father loves and pities his children, so the Lord loves and pities those who fear Him [with reverence, worship, and awe].—Psalm 103:8–13 AMP

The past is gone forever if you have confessed your sins and failures to the Lord Jesus. That 1DAAT truth can set you free!

CRSO

Many days when I start to feel fear, I'll stop and think, "What am I fearing?"

Almost always I will then realize that I am fearing what I have to do tomorrow or next week, and God is not with me in this picture. I will catch myself thinking about how it's all going to work out and the details. I'm not living one day at a time. I'm bringing into today what I might do tomorrow or the next day. That is causing me to fear.

When I am not living in the present, I'm usually living in regret or fear—specifically regrets of the past or fear of the future.

All of my life, even as a Christian, I had never realized what living one day at a time *really* meant. Knowing this has caused such a profound effect on me.

I must only live for today. I cannot worry about what will happen tomorrow. That doesn't mean that I can't pray about things in the future or plan for what I need to do tomorrow. God wants us to be wise and prudent, but I have to give troublesome situations to Him. I cannot worry about tomorrow.

I know this is what Jesus referred to in the Bible. It doesn't mean that I don't have trials and tribulations, but

I'm learning through such practical advice from my brother, such practical, every day, down-to-earth things.

I realize more than ever that when I am worrying about the future, God is never in the picture.

As a result, I now live in a peace that I never knew before. I experience joy so much deeper than I ever knew before.

Because of God's grace and mercy, I am getting better about not bringing in to today what I might do tomorrow and not worrying about the future.

And I learned that 1DAAT truth from a man who had to hit bottom before he discovered how God could change him one day at a time!

My brother would not have been considered spiritually-minded by many Christians, nor by myself when we first started our special conversations, yet I discovered in the process that he had the strongest faith and the most peace of anybody I've ever known.

CONVERSATIONS AND REFLECTIONS

When people are not living in the present, it is usually because they are living in regret or fear—specifically regrets of the past or fear of the future. What are your greatest regrets and fears? How can 1DAAT living help you face these?

_____

_____

_____

_____

_____

_____

To personalize, write the words to 1 John 4:18 in your own words:

_____

_____

_____

PRAYER TO LIVE ONE DAY AT A TIME

Dear Lord, help me to focus on You, not my fears. I must only live for today. I cannot worry about what will happen tomorrow. I know that You want me to be wise, so I will pray about things in the future, and I will plan for what I need to do tomorrow. Still, I willingly give troublesome situations to You, rather than worrying about them. Amen.

12

SMALL MIRACLES: February 19, 2004

You are the God who performs miracles; you display
your power among the peoples. — Psalm 77:14

Thursday morning, February 19, I felt led to pick up
the telephone and call Richard. Just as passing conversation, I told my brother about something small that had
recently happened in my life.

"It wasn't that big of a deal," I said. "Maybe it was just a
coincidence, but to me it was a real blessing."

He paused a moment, then he offered, "There are no
coincidences in life. They are actually small miracles where
God chooses to remain anonymous."

He mentioned once again how important it was to turn
your life and will over to God, then to be willing to accept
the outcome, but we didn't talk long.

CBEO

That conversation, short and sweet, was much more eye-opening than I had imagined it would be. From that day, I began to see in brand new ways how life is chock-filled with small miracle after small miracle.

The fact that God really cares about me was no new concept. I knew that He loved me long before Richard and I began to talk a few times a month. Where I had missed it before was not seeing that I was important enough to receive these little "kisses on the cheek" from God.

Best of all, I know now that there are no small miracles. Some miracles I have received since this particular conversation with Richard I hardly consider small. In many ways, all miracles are huge because we know from Whom they come. I don't want to ever take miracles—large or small—for granted, nor do I call them coincidences anymore!

Albert Einstein said: "There are two ways to live your life—one is as though nothing is a miracle, the other is as though everything is a miracle."

Since that short conversation on February 19 with my brother, I have chosen to live as though *everything* is a miracle. I can't fathom the alternative.

CBEO

Living that way is not Fantasyland. In many ways, it is a heightened awareness of reality—what is real and what is not.

You hear of so many people who go through horrible situations, yet they emerge with story after story of miracles. Perhaps this occurs because when you get in those horrible situations, all of the so-called spiritual bull is gone. It is just you and God. All the pious phrases vanish. You have to live in reality. And you get to see God's miracles in the smallest of things.

I was reminded of this, and of Richard's words about "small miracles," as I read *Return with Honor* (Doubleday, 1995) by Captain Scott O'Grady. He was a Christian and a United States Air Force captain whose F-16 jet was shot down by a Bosnian Serb SA-6 on June 2, 1995, while he was patrolling the no-fly zone.

He ejected and came to earth near Mrkonjić Grad in Serb-held territory. Scott survived for six days eating leaves, grass, and insects while avoiding Serb patrols who were intent on finding him. Meanwhile he kept trying to contact NATO's airborne command center. Miraculously, he evaded capture and was rescued six days later on June 8 by United States Marines.

I heard him speak about his experiences on talk-shows. At the time of greatest crisis, he suddenly realized why he had learned survival skills, why this bug was okay to eat and this one was not, how to live when all the human protection was gone.

No one likes the preparation, especially when it involves pushing-the-edge survival training, but that training often opens the door for the Lord's power to come rushing through.

During one particularly harrowing time as he hid from his captors his lips were chapped and he described his tongue as "a dry slab in my mouth." He desperately needed water. He was left with one option—pray! He asked God for a "cloud burst, for a downpour!" That evening it rained a soaking thunderstorm that wouldn't stop!

That's reality. He was in dire straits. He wasn't living in denial. He wasn't living in Fantasyland, yet when miracle after miracle came his way, he knew from Whom those blessings came.

 CREO

Likewise, I remember hearing an illustration of this guy who was caught in a flood. He climbed up on his roof and began to pray for a miracle.

A guy came by on a boat and shouted, "Can I help you?"

"No, I'm asking God for a miracle."

Another guy came by on a raft and yelled, "Can I help you?"

"No," the man sitting on the house called back. "I'm asking God for a miracle."

Then a helicopter flew overhead. The would-be rescuer broadcast over a bullhorn, "Can we help you?"

"No," the man on the house shouted back as he waved the helicopter away, trying to be heard over the chopper's noise, "I'm asking God for a miracle!"

According to the story, the man kept praying and claiming God's promises for safety and help. Finally he got fed up with praying and exclaimed, "God, why won't You rescue me?"

To which God replied, "I've sent a raft, a boat and a helicopter, and you keep sending them away!"

෬෫෮

After this conversation with my brother, I began to realize how many times the Bible mentions how God has worked miracles in the lives of His people. Here are a few for study and meditation:

He performs wonders that cannot be fathomed, miracles that cannot be counted. —Job 9:10

I will remember the deeds of the LORD; yes, I will remember your miracles of long ago.—Psalm 77:11

You are the God who performs miracles; you display your power among the peoples.—Psalm 77:14

Remember the wonders he has done, his miracles.— Psalm 105:5

God loves to perform miracles. He is the God of making the impossible possible every day, for Jesus promised, "With man this is impossible, but with God all things are possible" (Matthew 19:26). He is a God of pure love and goodness. It is up to us to recognize His hand in our lives.

CONVERSATIONS AND REFLECTIONS

Richard said, "There are no coincidences in life. They are actually small miracles where God chooses to remain anonymous." Looking back over the past weeks and months, what are some of the "small miracles" that you have seen in your life?

To personalize, write the words to Job 9:10 in your own words:

_____

_____

_____

_____

PRAYER OF APPRECIATION

Dear Lord, thank You for caring for me. Help me to see in brand new ways how my life has been filled with "small miracle" after "small miracle." I'm sorry for ignoring too many times that You love me and that I'm important enough to receive Your little "kisses on the cheek." I give You all the glory for everything You have done in my life. Help me to continue to see Your hand in my life today and tomorrow. Amen.

13

TWO MISTAKES:
March 9, 2004

"Surely God is my salvation; I will trust and not be afraid. The LORD, the LORD, is my strength and my song; he has become my salvation." —Isaiah 12:2

One of the greatest challenges for me was facing my fears. No matter how good I felt I was doing, as I tried to learn what God was teaching me through conversations with my brother, something would happen, and I would find myself plunging right back into fear.

I honestly did not know what I was going to do with my life, nor did I know whether I would be able to pay my bills. I sometimes found myself fearful of the future.

I didn't want to think about divorce, about being single again at sixty. I had done it at forty, and here I was facing it all over again.

It didn't take a lot sometimes to push me over the edge into fear. Fear doesn't have to be rational. In fact, it usually isn't.

It isn't rational that many Holocaust survivors, long after being freed from the Nazi concentration camps, sometimes lived in fear of being imprisoned again in another concentration camp. But all it took was for some small smell or sound to trigger a painful memory and all the fears and feelings returned.

It isn't rational that a physical abuse victim, long after he or she has been separated from a cruel abuser, can hear a simple remark or spot an innocent gesture, and the overwhelming black hole of abuse seems to be swallowing them again.

It isn't rational that a soldier, long removed from combat, wakes up every night in the midst of a reoccurring nightmare, fearful of impending death for himself and his comrades. Still, I have heard stories of many whose fathers, brothers, spouses, or friends live otherwise normal lives, yet their nights are regularly spent returning to some far off jungle or desert. The fears, for these people, are just as real as life itself, at least for a few brief moments.

Now, I'm not saying that my fears were as ravaging as a Holocaust survivor's, an abuse victim's, or a war-hardened soldier's, but my fears were just as real to me.

C3ЪО

It was Tuesday, March 9, when the next early morning phone conversation took place.

"What's going on in your life?" my brother asked.

"It seems like everything is ripping apart," I said. I described the ugly situation I faced.

"Patti," Richard said after listening to me express my anxious thoughts, "let me tell you about two mistakes that I have made."

That got my attention, even though I had a sneaking suspicion that his "two mistakes" would point to my own challenges.

"First of all," he continued, "the first mistake has been wanting people to take my side. You've got to remember to let everyone else that you know be neutral. You can't expect people to take your side. People have a right to think what they want to think. You have to let others be neutral."

I didn't really like what he was saying, but I kept listening. Quickly he went to the other of the two mistakes.

My brother said, "Expectations are planned disappointments."

ഇൽ

I had hoped that Richard would spend more time talking about expectations, the second mistake. He didn't elaborate that day, though he did soon after that. We said good-bye, and before we talked again, the storms continued to swirl around me. The tension grew by the day.

ଔଥ

Three days later, on March 12, 2004, as I spent time with the Lord, I heard Him speak clearly to me—"Patti, stay in My presence and I will make things happen the way they are supposed to happen."

Just a few simple words direct from my brother's heart had been more effective in opening my heart to hear God's leading than any polished speech or sermon.

I only hoped to survive the coming days to see what God had in store.

CONVERSATIONS AND REFLECTIONS

If "expectations are planned disappointments," how have you set yourself up in the past for frustration and disillusionment? How can you live more effectively?

_____

_____

_____

_____

_____

_____

To personalize, write the words to 2 Corinthians 4:17 in your own words:

_____

_____

_____

_____

PRAYER OF APPRECIATION

Dear Lord, help me to stop expecting people to take my side. Help me to realize that expectations are planned disappointments. Thank You, God, for patiently guiding my life, even when I don't understand that You are working in my life for my good. Help me leave the outcome to You, for You always know what is best for me. Amen.

14

PAIN:
March 13, 2004

Consider it pure joy, my brothers, whenever you
face trials of many kinds, because you know that the
testing of your faith develops perseverance. — James
1:2-3

As I went through the pressure and turmoil taking place
as the season of conversations with Richard continued, I was completely alone, which — as I have mentioned
before — allowed me to spend hour after hour with my Lord
Jesus.

I simply stayed in the Bible. I cried. I prayed. I asked
God to help me. And out of the pit, He heard my cry for help
and for wisdom. All the time He was waiting for the right
moment when He would direct my brother Richard to call.

I described in my journal the pain I felt. It was an actual, physical pain. It was so bad that my internal organs hurt. I wrote:

I am hurting physically from this turmoil. Betrayal, lies, accusations, blame, fear, gossip and not knowing what's next, are physically weighing me down. I am numb. My insides hurt. I can't think straight. I choose to trust You, Lord. I choose to believe You, Lord. I will not turn back. I'm going forward with You. Help me.

Cঞর

By our fourteenth conversation on Saturday morning, March 13, 2004, the pain's intensity had reached new heights. In the midst of the worst of times, I talked to my brother about it and what I was trying to do to cope.

"I just want to get rid of the pain," I told Richard. "I'm hurting. My insides are aching. What's wrong with me that I can't get rid of it? I've been spending hours with the Lord. I've been learning so much from the conversations with you. But I can't seem to shake this pain."

That's when my brother said to me, "Patti, sometimes you can't get rid of it. You have to go through it. You can't run from it."

That stopped me cold. I didn't want to hear this. I wanted the pain to be gone. I wanted to quote the verse from 1 Peter 5:7 (KJV)—"Casting all your care upon him; for he careth for you." Then I wanted all my cares and pain to vanish immediately. I didn't want to go through it. I absolutely, positively wanted to run from what I was feeling.

Richard continued, "I've found that my pain comes from the uncertainty of not knowing how something is going to turn out. Here's the deal: It's okay to be in pain. You just have to go through it. You will eventually come out of it."

I felt like I was hearing a "no pain, no gain" line from some old exercise video.

Still, I knew inwardly that God had once again poured out a truth through Richard, and it could change my life if I would make the decision to follow what He was teaching me.

"Sometimes there is no way to get rid of the pain," he added for emphasis. "Remember that your pain is coming from not knowing how it is going to turn out. That is okay. But if you sit around and wallow in this, and if you don't allow God to lead you through the pain, you are going to be miserable much longer. Your own will is going to tell you that you are weak and that you should give up, but letting God lead you through the pain is surrendering to a Power that is greater than yourself. That's what God wants."

Once again I was awed at what he was saying, especially knowing from whom this was coming—a recovering alcoholic who had been through much pain and sorrow himself. I also reminded myself that God had seen fit to give him a glimpse of heaven as I listened to him share some of the most powerful, life-changing principles I had ever heard.

CЗ८О

After our conversation, I made several conscious decisions as I prepared to take my own trek through the pain.

One thing I did was spend some of my precious cash on a CD player that had a changer with five slots. I played praise and worship music in my house constantly, day and night. The CD player was in the central hallway, and music filled the air all the time.

As I've mentioned, I was all alone by this time, so it didn't bother anyone else. I could literally surround myself with worship, as the psalmist David wrote:

> But as for me, I will come into thy house in the multitude of thy mercy: and in thy fear will I worship toward thy holy temple. Lead me, O Lord, in thy righteousness because of mine enemies; make thy way straight before my face." —Psalm 5:7-8 kjv

I also made a conscious choice: "Okay, Lord, I'm going to go through this pain. I'm not going to run from it. I'm not going to try to get rid of it. I'm not going to keep crying out to you to release me from it."

I lay on the carpet on my stomach with my two arms stretched out over my head on the floor. I felt as if my hands were locked onto the ankles of Jesus, and I was going through a storm, like the winds were battering me, but I was going to hang onto Him. I wasn't letting go.

It is as real today as when it happened. When I got exhausted I was weak, but I knew I was going to make it. I knew it was a maturing process that I had never gone through before.

Until this time, any time I felt pain, I wanted to run to the Lord and ask Him to take the burdens off of me and onto Him, so I could be full of joy and peace. I thought that was what I was supposed to do.

What I experienced after that March 13 conversation with Richard was different. Jesus was teaching me that I was becoming more mature, that I would have to suffer and experience pain. It was simply part of the process.

"I'm not going to run from the pain," I vowed. "I won't be a little crybaby. I'm going to live through this. And I'm going to have to go through it, no matter how it feels."

I had to ask myself, "Am I willing to trust God in the midst of immense, intense pain?" The answer was "Yes!"

CRWO

I wish I could gloss over what happened next, but the pain didn't leave immediately. In some ways it got worse before it finally got better.

But God was doing something new as I learned what it meant to go through pain and accept it, and I found Scripture after Scripture on this often-neglected subject:

> We ought always to thank God for you, brothers, and rightly so, because your faith is growing more and more, and the love every one of you has for each other is increasing. Therefore, among God's churches we boast about your perseverance and faith in all the persecutions and trials you are enduring. All this is evidence that God's judgment is right, and as a result you will be counted worthy of the kingdom of God, for which you are suffering. — 2 Thessalonians 1:3-5

> Consider it pure joy, my brothers, whenever you face trials of many kinds, because you know that the testing of your faith develops perseverance. — James 1:2-3

> Praise be to the God and Father of our Lord Jesus Christ! In his great mercy he has given us new birth into a living hope through the resurrection of Jesus Christ from the dead, and into an inheritance that can never perish, spoil or fade — kept in heaven for

you, who through faith are shielded by God's power until the coming of the salvation that is ready to be revealed in the last time. In this you greatly rejoice, though now for a little while you may have had to suffer grief in all kinds of trials. These have come so that your faith—of greater worth than gold, which perishes even though refined by fire—may be proved genuine and may result in praise, glory and honor when Jesus Christ is revealed. —1 Peter 1:3-7

I would sometimes get into my car with my Bible and I would go out to a favorite park. I would just sit there. I've always enjoyed being outdoors, and I've always loved to walk, but during this time, I was in too much pain to walk a lot. I would just sit in my car for hours with the Lord. His presence was in that car. He was with me. I would read my Bible. I would write things down in my journal. I'd be out there two or three hours at a time.

More than anything, I became acutely aware that Christ Jesus had gone through the ultimate pain for my salvation:

Therefore, since we are surrounded by such a great cloud of witnesses, let us throw off everything that hinders and the sin that so easily entangles, and let us run with perseverance the race marked out for us. Let us fix our eyes on Jesus, the author and perfecter of our faith, who for the joy set before him endured the cross, scorning its shame, and sat down at the right hand of the throne of God. Consider him who endured such opposition from sinful men, so that you will not grow weary and lose heart.—Hebrews 12:1-3

How could I do anything less than endure the pain and hurt of my puny-by-comparison problems?

It was an eye-opening experience as I came to realize a greater depth of the Christian walk, one that required much more than I was previously willing to endure.

I look back on it, and it was a wonderful, sweet time of preparation for what was to come. It just didn't feel so wonderful or sweet at the time.

Life has gotten a lot busier since, but I'm so grateful for the privilege of being driven into the arms of Jesus during the time I was having these conversations with my brother.

I'm so appreciative that I was able to spend hours with the Lord—giving Him my undivided attention, even as I felt that He was giving me His undivided attention for hours a day, week after week. During those hours and days I learned to accept pain, endure the pain, walk though the pain, and learn that God was in control to heal in His time and in His way.

And I am eternally grateful for a brother who said so simply and clearly, "It's okay to be in pain. You just have to go through it. You will eventually come out of it."

CONVERSATIONS AND REFLECTIONS

Pain comes from the uncertainty of not knowing how something is going to turn out. What challenges are you facing that are causing pain? Specifically, how can you turn those uncertainties and challenges over to God?

_____

_____

_____

_____

_____

To personalize, write the words to 1 Peter 5:7 in your own words:

_____

_____

_____

_____

PRAYER OF APPRECIATION

Dear Lord, help me to realize that sometimes I can't get rid of all pain. Help me to go through it, rather than always wanting to run from hard trials. I cast all my care upon You. I cast all my uncertainties upon You, knowing that it is okay if I feel pain. I know that with Your help, I will come out of my challenges as pure gold. Amen.

15

RENT FREE:
March 24, 2004

The mind controlled by the Spirit is life and peace. —
Romans 8:6

Wednesday, March 24, 2004. The tension continued
to grow on all fronts. I mentioned this to my brother
as he asked about what was happening.

"Don't let human beings live rent free in your head,"
Richard said bluntly.

I asked him to explain.

He said, "When you have fear or other negative emotions in your head about someone else, you are letting them
live 'rent free' in your head. The more you try to fix things,
the more vulnerable you are. Do what's right, then leave it
up to God."

I kept writing furiously so I could go back through it afterward. He kept speaking in that familiar Midwest drawl: "There isn't a thing you can do about other people and what they do. They are the ones making choices and you can't do anything about it. Have no expectations. Quit trying to control. If you have expectations, you will be miserable all the time."

CRXO

After our good-byes, I thought, "There was that part about expectations again." I kept hoping he would explain more. (He did).

But the part about letting people live rent free in my head was something unique. I don't think I had ever heard that phrase before, but it made such sense the very first time my brother said it.

As usual, I spent a lot of time going through the Scriptures that God led me to, including these:

Since, then, you have been raised with Christ, set your hearts on things above, where Christ is seated at the right hand of God. Set your minds on things above, not on earthly things. — Colossians 3:1-2

For though we live in the world, we do not wage war as the world does. The weapons we fight with are not the weapons of the world. On the contrary, they have divine power to demolish strongholds. We demolish arguments and every pretension that sets itself up against the knowledge of God, and we take captive every thought to make it obedient to Christ. — 2 Corinthians 10:3-5

For the wisdom of this world is foolishness in God's sight. As it is written: "He catches the wise in their craftiness," and again, "The Lord knows that the thoughts of the wise are futile."—1 Corinthians 3:19-20

The mind of sinful man is death, but the mind controlled by the Spirit is life and peace. — Romans 8:6

Finally, brothers, whatever is true, whatever is noble, whatever is right, whatever is pure, whatever is lovely, whatever is admirable — if anything is excellent or praiseworthy — think about such things. — Philippians 4:8

 CB&O

It is apparent, even today, when I am obsessed with thoughts of another person, my mind is not set on things of God. Likewise, when my mind is constantly thinking about myself and my own challenges, this self-centered thinking is hardly what God wants me to do.

I am, as Richard so uniquely expressed it, giving away rent free the occupancy of my mind.

I am supposed to be talking to God, not myself. I need to focus on Him, not filling my mind with thoughts of others who seek to manipulate and control or are not doing things the way I think they should be done.

Reasoning, plotting, and planning are from my flesh and not the spirit. I am to be controlled by the Spirit, not my own head or mind.

Though we live in the world, we do not wage war as the world does. What a mighty, practical truth!

And what a burden is lifted when you evict those who want to live rent free!

This lesson, spoken during the fifteenth special conversation with my brother would make an amazing difference during the coming days.

CONVERSATIONS AND REFLECTIONS

Specifically, how have you let people live rent free in your head? What can you do to avoid the rent free challenge?

_____

_____

_____

_____

To personalize, write the words to Romans 8:6 in your own words:

PRAYER OF TRUST

Dear Lord, help me to stop letting people live rent free in my head. My expectations have often left me miserable. Help me to stop trying to fix things for everyone and continuing to make myself vulnerable to circumstances and people. Help me to do what is right and leave the outcome up to You as I learn to trust You more and more every day. Amen.

16

MOVING ON:
April 1, 2004

I do not consider, brethren, that I have captured and
made it my own [yet]; but one thing I do [it is my one
aspiration]: forgetting what lies behind and straining
forward to what lies ahead. — Philippians 3:13 AMP

Thursday, April's Fool Day, 2004.
"You don't have to hurt over this," Richard said as we
began our sixteenth special conversation. He was referring
to another family member who was causing me pain.

"It's been a very testing time," I related to my brother. "I
don't want to lose my relationship with them. I don't want to
reach the point where it is unfixable."

"You don't have to hurt over this," my brother repeated.

In a previous conversation, he had pointed to the need
for going through pain when the occasion called for it. In

this case, he was saying that I didn't have to hurt. I was a little puzzled.

He continued, "If you want to continue in a relationship with people, do it. Be open with your feelings. All you need to do is to stand up for what's right. What is important for you to do is to be honest and do what is right, then move on. Stop hurting and move on with your life."

I hardly had time to write and digest that idea before he moved back into a mention of the rent free discussion and more.

"Remember how I said that I don't let human beings live rent free in my head?" he asked. "When I have emotions or fear in my head because of what someone else did, I'm letting them live rent free. The more I try to fix things, the more vulnerable I am. I do what's right. I leave it up to God. And I go on with God. There isn't a thing I can do about other people and what they do. They have to make their own choices, and I can't do anything about it. I can't have expectations about them. If I do, I will be miserable all the time."

I jotted notes in my journal hastily.

Then he added, "You can't do anything about people, places or things, so quit trying."

৫৪৪০

"Patti," Richard changed directions, "you need to sit down and make a gratitude list. Quit feeling sorry for yourself. Don't get in a pity party. Start writing things down that are blessing you today."

Another arrow straight to the heart! Even though I had been talking about a number of things that were causing tension, it must have come through loud and clear that I was simply sulking.

It was true. I kept trying to put on a fresh face with a stiff upper lip, so to speak, but I was going through a lot of despair. I didn't know my future.

Regardless, after I got off the telephone, I got a notebook and started writing a gratitude list. Day after day I wrote all the things I was grateful for, even down to hearing the train whistle blow in my Dallas suburb . . . the birds singing . . . a phone call from a friend who cared enough to call and wish me a good day . . . hot water . . . a car to drive . . . food on the table . . . clean drinking water . . . air to breathe . . . a place to call home . . . family . . . friends . . . faith.

Then an interesting thing happened—as I looked through my gratitude book, I started seeing the hand of God in my life. Everything began taking on a much different perspective.

There is an old illustration about someone who watched a tapestry maker working. It seemed like such a mishmash of colors and fabrics. Nothing made sense. Then the worker turned the tapestry over and a beautiful picture was revealed.

My gratitude book helped me see what God was already seeing. What a different picture!

In Texas there's a phrase about pulling yourself up by your bootstraps. The gratitude book pulled me up. And I have kept giving God the gift of a grateful heart. I am grateful for all the wonderful things in the universe and for all the blessings in my life.

႙ဢ

I wrote these words in my journal: "I prayed for the situations that are causing such turmoil, and I laid everything at the feet of Jesus. I said, 'Thy will be done.' I have to let go of any conflicts and move on."

႙ဢ

And then God's hand moved within the conflict. He turned what had been the age-old paradox of "the unstoppable force meeting the unmovable object" with this family member into a realization that everyone involved benefited from leaving the conflict behind and putting together a workable solution. God worked everything out—it seems like such a trite, simple phrase, but it brought resolution and harmony to the situation.

That, to me, is a major miracle!

All that I was learning through my brother was hardly a class in theory. I was getting to live it out in a very real world. I was in the midst of major life decisions and felt as if the pressure cooker called life was plopped on an intensifying fire.

Then God stepped in! Again and again.

CONVERSATIONS AND REFLECTIONS

List several things about which you are grateful, and how the entries on your gratitude list have positively changed your life.

_____

_____

_____

_____

_____

To personalize, write the words to Philippians 4:13 in your own words:

_____

_____

_____

_____

PRAYER FOR MOVING ON

Dear Lord, help me to understand that I can't do anything about the choices that other people make. I can't do anything about people, places or things. I can't have expectations about them, or I will be miserable. Help me to see that when I have emotions or fear, I am giving control to others. Help me to be grateful. I choose to place my life and my future in Your hands. I trust You. Your will be done! Amen.

17

NEED:
April 5, 2004

I am with you and will watch over you wherever you go, and I will bring you back to this land. I will not leave you until I have done what I have promised you. —Genesis 28:15

Monday, April 5, 2004.

"You need to do what you can do for yourself," Richard said in our seventeenth special conversation. "You cannot control others. You cannot control the outcome."

I got it. It wasn't a matter of being selfish. Far from it. What he was saying pointed to the fact that I could only make decisions for myself, with God's guidance and with peace as my umpire. And then I had to trust the Lord for the results.

"Patti," Richard repeated again, "say 'Dear God, I turn this situation over to You, and whatever happens, I know it is your will. The timetable is up to You. The results are up to You.' You see, I have found that if I have truly turned my life and my will over to God, then I should relax because I'm not in control."

လ၃ၷ

It was a major decision to take my hands off of my life and stop trying to control everything and everyone involved. It was also a continual decision, as I kept wanting to take control back.

Was I ever going to learn this lesson?

God kept proving Himself faithful, but only after I got out of His way.

And I kept discovering more and more verses that put the entire principle of control in a completely new perspective, including "Unto You, O Lord, do I bring my life."—Psalm 25:1 AMP

In my case, only when I eventually got so weary of trying to manage and control my own life did I hand it over to God. When I did, I began to experience the abundant, joyful, and fruitful life that Jesus promised: "The thief cometh not, but for to steal, and to kill, and to destroy: I am come that they might have life, and that they might have it more abundantly."—John 10:10 KJV

Unfortunately, many people seem afraid of totally surrendering their lives to God, because they think He will reduce them to some drab, dreary life. That is not what the Bible teaches: Psalm 37:4 promises, "Delight yourself in the Lord and He will give you the desires of your heart." God is not interested in making you miserable. He is interested in bringing to life the dreams and desires He has placed inside you, and even more. He is even more eager to see the abundant life come to pass in your life than you are, but it requires handing over the reins of your life to Him.

I have also found that many people are reluctant to surrender their lives because they don't really believe that His plans for them are actually better than their own.

I was certainly like that!

Truth is, the Lord created us with specific plans and purposes in mind, and there is simply no way we could improve upon them, as Jeremiah 29:11 tells us — "'For I know the plans I have for you,' declares the Lord, 'plans to prosper you and not to harm you, plans to give you hope and a future.'"

God's plans are good plans, the best plans, but we can only begin to see them unfold as we put our agendas aside and submit to His.

The Bible declares, "Since He did not spare even His own Son for us but gave Him up for us all, won't He also surely give us everything else?" — Romans 8:32 (TLB)

No matter where you are in your walk with the Lord Jesus, if you are still holding onto the reins of your life, there is no better time to surrender all that you are and all that you have to the Lord. Only then will you begin to live the adventurous, abundant life that belongs to you in Christ, for "No eye has seen, no ear has heard, no mind has conceived what God has prepared for those who love Him."—1 Corinthians 2:9

CONVERSATIONS AND REFLECTIONS

Specifically, what has kept you from unconditionally surrendering your will, life and future to God?

_____

_____

_____

_____

_____

To personalize, write the words to Jeremiah 29:11 in your own words:

_____

_____

_____

_____

PRAYER OF CONTINUED SURRENDER

Dear God, help me to continue to turn every situation in my life over to You, knowing that whatever happens, I know it is Your will. I know the plans that You have for me, to prosper me and not harm me, to give me hope and a future. The results are up to You. Amen.

18

EXPECTATIONS: June 7, 2004

Therefore, since we have been justified through faith, we have peace with God through our Lord Jesus Christ, through whom we have gained access by faith into this grace in which we now stand. And we rejoice in the hope of the glory of God. Not only so, but we also rejoice in our sufferings, because we know that suffering produces perseverance; perseverance, character; and character, hope. And hope does not disappoint us, because God has poured out his love into our hearts by the Holy Spirit, whom he has given us. —Romans 5:1-5

By midyear 2004, I had survived six months of a surreal world, yet God had worked challenge after challenge out.

Then my twelve year old grandson Keylan almost died. He was such a healthy boy, the pitcher on his baseball team. He had never gone through any physical problems much, but he began mentioning that it was hurting when he was breathing. He was taken to the doctor, but nothing was found. Three times during two months he woke up with his chest hurting a lot, and his parents rushed him to the emergency room where his lungs and heart were checked, then he was sent home. His discomfort was attributed to growing pains.

At school one day Keylan told his teacher that he wasn't feeling well, so he was sent to the nurse's office. He went into the bathroom close by, but he never came out. When someone went in to check on him, he had totally passed out, lying in a pool of sweat and white as a sheet, even his lips.

My daughter Natalie was called. For some reason she had not gone to her office but was working from home that day, only five minutes from the school (compared to twenty-five minutes between the school and her business).

Natalie rushed him to the nearest children's hospital. Keylan's doctor had already called the hospital, so heart surgeons were waiting for my daughter Natalie's car. Keylan's white lips let them know that something was wrong with his heart.

A man who had previously been their neighbor was the on-call emergency room pediatrician, and he took control and got Keylan inside.

Keylan went into congestive heart failure. He was in the intensive care unit for three days. They did all the tests for viral and bacterial infections but everything looked normal.

"On paper," the doctors agreed, "he looks like the healthiest kid around."

They explained that there are only two things that cause congestive heart failure in a twelve-year-old: a traumatic accident with a blow to the chest, or a major infection that affects the heart, causing it to protect itself by building fluid up in the pericardium sac around the heart. The latter was obviously what had happened, but the physicians couldn't figure out what was causing the infection.

Puzzled, the hospital brought in four different infectious disease doctors, testing for a rare virus or bacteria he might have contracted. Everything turned out normal, yet fluid kept building around his heart. The attendants, even with the latest equipment, were barely keeping him alive.

Medications seemed to make things better, so they eventually let him go home. Quickly, however, the condition worsened and he was rushed back to the hospital.

The doctors at the children's hospital wanted to go in and cut a hole in the pericardium sac to drain the fluid and test a piece of the sac to see what they could find.

His parents prayed, seeking guidance about the cardiologist they would use. The one chosen proved to be the difference, and the miracles that followed were truly extraordinary.

During exploratory surgery the cardiologist discovered that the pericardium was so thick it was choking the heart, and that Keylan, under the best of circumstances and medicines, would not have lived more than a few years.

We were told later that a thickened pericardium cannot be detected through current tests, but only through surgery. Only because of the infection and fluid did they go inside; otherwise they would never have known.

During the open-heart surgery that followed, the front part of the pericardium sac was removed, which drained the fluid. The thickness of the remainder of the sac was removed, as well.

Since then, Keylan's health has been wonderful. Today he is a growing teenager. If you saw him, you would never know he ever faced a life-threatening illness.

God is good!

ೞ

There was no writing in my journal or any more conversations with my brother until June 7, 2004. Then, on that day, I wrote in my journal,

Keylan was very sick and almost died. What a trial and a walk of faith. I saw Natalie take care of Keylan in the most beautiful way, and I'm so proud of the wonderful mother she is.

And on that Monday morning, I heard the now-familiar Missouri drawl on the phone line. He sounded weak, but it was so good to hear his voice.

So much had gone on during the time between our seventeenth and this eighteenth conversation. As usual, he cut to the proverbial chase: "Expectations are planned disappointments."

He had told me that before. I was glad that he had brought it up again. I wanted to know more. He didn't disappoint.

"If you want to have planned disappointments," he continued, "then just expect."

Again, I wrote every word down, waiting for him to say more.

"I've learned I cannot control people, places or things," he said. "I don't have that power. I've turned my life and my will over to God, and I don't have any expectations."

ɔ୫ଠ

I got off the phone and gave every expectation I had to God in prayer. I didn't really understand the concept, "no expectations," so I had to accept it by faith.

Since that time, I have learned that there is a major difference between hope and expectations. There can be a demanding aspect to expectations, and that is what my brother was referring to. On the other hand, hope suggests confidence and assurance that God knows best. I have hope because of God's promises to me throughout the Bible, including these:

May the God of hope fill you with all joy and peace as you trust in him, so that you may overflow with hope by the power of the Holy Spirit.—Romans 15:13

Command those who are rich in this present world not to be arrogant nor to put their hope in wealth, which is so uncertain, but to put their hope in God, who richly provides us with everything for our enjoyment.—1 Timothy 6:17

"For I know the plans I have for you," declares the LORD, "plans to prosper you and not to harm you, plans to give you hope and a future."—Jeremiah 29:11

The LORD will guide you always; he will satisfy your needs in a sun-scorched land and will strengthen your frame. You will be like a well-watered garden, like a spring whose waters never fail.—Isaiah 58:11

However, I cannot base the future on my own expectations, not if I have surrendered totally to God. I have learned that I can expect God to be who He says He is and to expect His promises to be true.

Since becoming a Christian, I realize it is impossible to live the Christian life in my own strength. God knows I can't do it by myself, and He has provided His life for me so I can.

Now, each morning I commit that day and myself and my will to Him. It is so wonderful to enter into intimate communion, fellowship, and friendship with God. Letting Him be the Lord of each day takes the tension out of my life and makes God responsible for getting me through the day. This is what He wants me to do. He wants to fellowship with each of His children, and wants each of us to spend time with Him.

My old self is dead (or at least dying!) and Jesus lives His life in me, as Paul declares in Galatians 2:20—"I have been crucified with Christ and I no longer live, but Christ lives in me. The life I live in the body, I live by faith in the Son of God, who loved me and gave himself for me."

During the day I commit each need to Him. I commit my interruptions to Him and let Him be Lord of them also.

C33&O

There wasn't a lot for kids to do where I grew up in our small hometown of three thousand people, so we had dances. My father was a square dance caller, so I went to a lot of the events with him and my mother, and I enjoyed square dancing.

When dancing (at least with the old school dances that I grew up with!), the male always leads. The female just relaxes and follows. When each does their part well, everything goes smoothly. But if the female tries to lead the dance, it becomes awkward, clumsy, bumpy, and not fun at all for either party.

I am not trying to be simplistic, but life has become like dancing. It only works well when I relax and follow Him. Everything works smoothly as long as I put my cheek against my Lord's cheek, rest in His arms and let Him lead the dance of my life, one day at a time!

My prayer is that you will learn this dance, too.

CONVERSATIONS AND REFLECTIONS

In your own words, what is the difference between hope and expectations? How can that difference impact your life and your walk with God?

_____

_____

_____

_____

_____

_____

To personalize, write the words to Romans 15:13 in your own words:

_____

_____

_____

_____

PRAYER OF APPRECIATION

Dear Lord, help me to understand the difference between hope and expectations. Help me to stop demanding with my expectations, and to have a hope that brings confidence and assurance that You always know best. I cast all my uncertainties, demands and unrealistic expectations upon You, and I claim hope that is based on Your promises throughout the Bible. Amen.

19

GRATITUDE:
August 16, 2004

Let the word of Christ dwell in you richly as you
teach and admonish one another with all wisdom, and
as you sing psalms, hymns and spiritual songs with
gratitude in your hearts to God. — Colossians 3:16

On August 13, 2004, I spoke briefly with Richard over
the telephone. He was having more heart problems,
and the outlook was not promising.

He was very weak, so I did most of the talking.

"Richard," I said as calmly as I could, "If you hadn't
been willing to talk to me and be honest with me and be a
vessel for God, all the good things I am now experiencing
would have never happened. You had to be willing, and I'll
always be grateful to you." I wanted Richard to know how
deeply his words had touched me.

On the phone, he never took any credit. He knew it was God. He knew it wasn't him. He was always very up front, never cut corners. He was honest and blunt. That's what I needed.

The next day, his heart failed, and he was put on life support. But he had gone without oxygen too long, and the decision was made to take him off life support.

As we had three years before, many family members headed for the Missouri hospital to say our good-byes.

On August 16, I was able to go into his ICU room and have one more conversation before he was unhooked from life support. He couldn't talk. I'm not even sure that he heard me, but I knew that I needed to say what was on my heart.

Mostly I stood by his bed and wept and sobbed profusely. I felt like I was losing my lifeline to God. I loved Richard so much.

Finally, through gut-wrenching sobs, I told him much the same as what I had said the previous Monday over the telephone.

"Thank you, thank you, thank you for listening to God and being a vessel to share what He wanted you to give me. Because of what you have done for me, my life will forever be better. I'm a changed person. I'm so grateful that you loved me enough to give me your wisdom and time. I love you, and I'll always be grateful to you."

CʒꙄ

Later that day I wrote a simple prayer in my journal:

Dear Lord, I pray for myself this morning. As I come before You humbly, acknowledging who You are, the only true God, the great I AM, I ask You what Jabez asked You in Your word: I cry out to You from the depths of my heart and ask that You would bless me and enlarge my life to serve You. I ask that Your hand might be with me and that You would keep me from evil so it might not hurt me. I lay this prayer at your feet and ask; "Thy will be done." Amen.

Then I wrote, "Richard died—August 16, 2004."

CONVERSATIONS AND REFLECTIONS

Name at least one person who has been used by God to bring greater insight into your life. How?

_____

_____

_____

_____

_____

To personalize, write the words to Psalm 37:23 in your own words:

_____

_____

_____

_____

PRAYER OF GRATITUDE

Dear Lord, I come before You humbly, acknowledging who You are, the only true God, the great I AM. I ask what Jabez asked you in Your word. I cry out to you from the depths of my heart and ask that You would bless me and enlarge my life to serve You. I ask that Your hand might be with me and that You would keep me from evil so it might not hurt me. I lay this prayer at your feet and ask; "Your will be done." Amen.

20

GOODBYE:
August 18, 2004

There is a time for everything, and a season for every activity under heaven: a time to be born and a time to die. —Ecclesiastes 3:1-2

Wednesday, August 18, 2004, I had one last chance to say my final goodbye.

The entombment took place at the Memorial Park Mausoleum in Cape Girardeau, Missouri, where he lived most of his adult life. He is buried in a granite mausoleum with a bronze plate simply inscribed:

1DAAT
MILLER
Richard E (Dick) 1937-2004

Mary, his widow, spoke of their love story at the funeral. His son, Steve, spoke wonderfully of his dad's life, mentioning their bond as father and son, and how they had been golf buddies. My daughter Natalie sang "The Lord's Prayer" beautifully.

More than five hundred people attended the visitation and service, a very large gathering for a small community. So many came up both before and afterward to say how much Richard had meant to them. In fact, I had spoken with a family physician and thanked him for all he had done for my brother, and he responded with tears brimming in his eyes, "You don't understand how much he helped me."

Another prominent man in the community came up to me and said, "I don't know what I'm going to do without him!"

Again and again people came up to me to tell me what Richard had meant to them and how he had impacted their lives.

೦೩೮೦

Though I had been invited to speak publicly at many events and meetings for more than thirty years, there was no way I could speak that day through my grief. Even though I had hardly known Richard three years before, with all that had happened, especially during the last six months of his life, the loss I felt was too overwhelming.

But after the service was over, even though I knew Richard's spirit was in heaven, I walked over to his mausoleum, reached out to the glistening granite surface, looked up at his inscribed name plate and held back my tears just long enough to say the words one more time that had ended each of our very special, life-changing telephone conversations.

"I love you. Goodbye."

Richard and Patti, December 28, 2003

CONVERSATIONS AND REFLECTIONS

If you could bring everything down to a few principles, what
have you learned while reading this book?

_____

_____

_____

_____

To personalize, write the words to Psalm 116:1-2 in your
own words:

_____

_____

_____

_____

PRAYER OF GRATITUDE

*Dear Lord, I ask for Your direction through every situation
that I face, both today and tomorrow. Help me to see Your
hand at work in every area of my life. Your will be done! I
choose to follow Your guidance, and I am grateful for everything that You are doing for my good. I love You. Amen*

Afterword

Then I saw a new heaven and a new earth, for the first heaven and the first earth had passed away, and there was no longer any sea. I saw the Holy City, the new Jerusalem, coming down out of heaven from God, prepared as a bride beautifully dressed for her husband. And I heard a loud voice from the throne saying, "Now the dwelling of God is with men, and he will live with them. They will be his people, and God himself will be with them and be their God. He will wipe every tear from their eyes. There will be no more death or mourning or crying or pain, for the old order of things has passed away."... .The twelve gates were twelve pearls, each gate made of a single pearl. The great street of the city was of pure gold, like transparent glass. I did not see a temple in the city, because the Lord God Almighty and the Lamb are its temple. —Revelation 21:1-4; 21-22

O n August 27, 2001, my brother slipped into a coma for the first time. Six days later he awakened in the Southeast Missouri Hospital Intensive Care Unit. When I was allowed to go in to spend ten minutes with him, he had startled me by saying, "I saw heaven! It's beautiful!"

He kept saying that over and over.

"It's beautiful! I saw this huge pearl gate. It's huge!"

He kept saying it: "It's beautiful! It's *beau*-tiful!"

He described the pearl gate again—"It's huge. *Huge!*"

That man lying in the bed was acting so differently from the brother I knew. Yet I felt the presence of God as he was sharing his truly remarkable experience. I felt as if I was standing on holy ground in that intensive care room.

Through his tears, he said, "I didn't see God, but He told me I had to go back because He has more work for me to do."

As I mentioned earlier, something had happened to my brother! I had prayed for him for years, and now God had let him see heaven! I was amazed.

०३४०

In the ensuing three years, we only talked a few times. I could see the difference at family gatherings when he prayed such pure prayers to a God whom he obviously knew intimately.

Yet there wasn't much else that I could see until we began our telephone conversations. Out of the blue, the early morning phone conversations began on December 9, 2003. Counting the time I spoke by phone with him just before the decision was made to remove his life support, we had eighteen phone conversations in a little more than eight months. They were brief phone calls. He said what he was supposed to say. Then I spent time with the Lord Jesus.

Even today, I remain amazed that the God of the universe cared enough about me to send Richard back to share these conversations with me. He knew I was going to need to hear him, such an unexpected voice in my life, speak so simply and clearly.

Cʒໄ

God did such a mighty, unexpected work in my heart as a result of these conversations with my brother. The Lord has taken away unforgiveness, bitterness, resentment, and negative thoughts against people who, as I see in retrospect, were part of the process to help me discover what God truly had in mind for me.

How can I judge people anymore, now that it has become so clear what Jesus has done for me? In fact, Jesus said:

DO NOT judge and criticize and condemn others, so that you may not be judged and criticized and condemned yourselves. For just as you judge and criticize and condemn others, you will be judged and criticized and condemned, and in accordance with the measure you [use to] deal out to others, it will be dealt out again to you. —Matthew 7:1-2 AMP

Jesus also said that He didn't come to earth to judge, so how can I? If anything, that is one of the greatest lessons I learned in the very special talks with Richard.

CBEO

I didn't write in my journal again until September 1, 2004, nearly a half-month after Richard's funeral. Finally I took out my journal and began penning these words:

I haven't been able to write in my journal for weeks. Thank You, Lord, for letting us keep Keylan with us on earth for awhile longer. Lord, Your goodness and Your love for me have been so overwhelming on a daily basis that there has been too much to even try to write. I understand why the apostle John wrote, "And there are also many other things which Jesus did. If they should be all recorded one by one [in detail], I suppose that even the world itself could not contain (have room for) the books that would be written" —John 21:25 AMP

Since I have written in my journal the last time, You decided to take my precious brother Richard home with you. Now he has no more pain, tears or sorrow, and he is playing golf on the most beautiful course in the entire heavens and earth. And I thank You, Lord, for speaking so clearly to me and guiding me since last December through Richard. What a treasure and legacy You have left through him in my life here on earth. The nuggets of gold are etched deeply on my heart, and I will forever hear Your voice speaking these words of wisdom through the conversations with my brother.

Forever!

Epilogue

Richard died in 2004, but our conversations continue to bear fruit in my life. The wisdom my loving brother imparted enables me to enjoy a remarkably different life now. I feel as if Jesus sits or stands nearby, rides in my car, and is beside me twenty-four hours a day, seven days a week. I have made progress, but I'm still learning every day.

Though it's not audible, I'm familiar with "the sound of His voice." I can sense His presence, His hugs, His encouragement, His guidance; and I "hear" when He tells me He loves me. I can sense when I am going in the wrong direction and that He wants me to turn another way. There are tender intimacies in the quiet times of communion with God. I stand in amazement at what God has done and have an incredible sense of humility for God's mercy and grace.

I respond to His love by giving Him my life and my will as often as I think of it throughout the day. I say, "Not my will but thine be done," and mean it with all my heart. He has captured my love and total devotion, because He loved me first and has gone out of His way to woo me.

I love my Lord and Savior more than I ever dreamed possible. And He continues to speak to me often.

One day, I, too, will see heaven—and I know who will be waiting for me at the "huge pearl gate!"

About the Author

Patti Miller Dunham has spoken at conferences, churches, retreats and business events for more than thirty years. She has taught women's Bible studies and has been dedicated to studying the Bible and to teaching and nurturing others in the Christian faith since she became a Christian in 1969.

Patti has founded two businesses: A national cosmetics company and an international professional photography supply company.

Patti has one lovely daughter, a handsome son-in-law and two wonderful grandsons. At the time of publishing, she also has the privilege of taking care of her precious, sweet, ninety-two year old mother who lives with her.

If you would like to contact Patti or request a speaking engagement for your group, please contact her at:

Patti Miller Dunham
PO Box 92662
Southlake, Texas 76092

Or send an email to: pattimillerdunham@me.com